D0064940

To:

_____

From:

_____

Acknowledgments

I have had the privilege of growing up around rather remarkable people:

My father, who was called by God for a unique worldwide ministry and who loved and prayed for me from a distance. He has established his own unique, loving legacy in my life.

My mother, who continues to pass on her legacy of love as I watch her example in adjusting to change. This book is my tribute to her.

My sisters, Anne and Gigi, and my brothers, Franklin and Ned, who share with me the legacy and joy of being Mother and Daddy's children.

There have been many contributors to this book, and I am so appreciative of them. I would like to extend special thanks to:

My Aunt Virginia Somerville for her diligent record keeping for our family.

Russ Busby for the years he has chronicled our lives in photographs.

Stacy Mattingly, who has envisioned and crafted the book you now hold in your hand. Her talent, attention to detail, and spiritual insights have brought this project to life.

Sara Dormon, my extraordinary friend and executive administrator; and Anne Frank, my executive assistant, who continues to brighten my life.

Wes Yoder, my agent, for his friendship, guidance, and excellent work; along with all the staff at Ambassador Agency.

Tom Dean, associate publisher of Inspirio, who has been a joy to work with—his enthusiasm has been a great encouragement along the way. I would also like to thank Amy Wenger, Inspirio product and design manager, for her excellence and creativity; as well as Kim Zeilstra, Inspirio assistant operations manager, who has done much of the administrative work for us; and Caroline Blauwkamp, Inspirio's very gracious Senior Vice President.

And finally, in loving memory of my mother's parents, L. Nelson and Virginia Bell, whose legacy lives on.

For Mother

Requests for information should be addressed to:
Inspirio, the gift group of Zondervan
Grand Rapids, Michigan 49530
http://www.inspiriogifts.com

www.ruthgrahamministries.com

Editor / Project Manager: Tom Dean
Design Manager: Amy J. Wenger
Art and Design: Koechel Peterson & Associates, Inc. Minneapolis, MN

Printed in China
05 06 07/LPC/ 4 3

A Legacy of Love

Things I Learned From My Mother

RUTH GRAHAM

Daughter of BILLY *and* RUTH GRAHAM
with STACY MATTINGLY

inspirio™

CHAPTER I

COUNTING THE HOURS THAT SHINE

Joy is the serious business of heaven.
C.S. LEWIS

DARKNESS CAME EARLY that December day. Winter had established itself in the mountains of North Carolina, and afternoon seemed to slip into evening with little warning. Hadn't I only just gotten home from school?

Now, standing at the bay window in the kitchen, a fire popping and crackling beside me in the big stone fireplace, I could no longer make out the few sentinel pine trees rising up from below the patch of lawn in front of the house, or the dark masses—the mountains—in the distance. The gray day had given way to a cold, black night. All I could see in the window was my reflection.

Behind me, Mother and Bea, our housekeeper, prepared my thirteenth birthday dinner of fried chicken. My grandparents, Nelson and Virginia Bell—whom we called *Lao E* and *Lao Niang*, our family's versions of the Chinese for grandfather and grandmother—had driven up from their house at the bottom of the mountain. Daddy was away but had phoned to wish me a happy birthday. He would be back in a few days—just in time for Christmas—and would bring my birthday gift with him.

The dining room table was beautifully set with Mother's china and silver and a holiday bouquet of flowers, probably sent to my parents by friends. I watched as Mother went back and forth between the dining room and kitchen, her heels clicking on the wood floor, her dark hair tucked behind her ear, and her eyes shining. Having finished our homework, my siblings and I moved into the living room and gathered around my grandparents, while pots and skillets rang under the skillful action of Bea's hands. The air was thick with the aromas of chicken, biscuits, and lemon cake, the menu I had selected for my birthday night.

BEGINNING AT THIRTEEN, MY FOUR SIBLINGS AND I RECEIVED SPECIAL GIFTS FROM MOTHER ON A FEW KEY BIRTHDAYS UNTIL WE TURNED TWENTY-ONE.

Thirteen was a special birthday in our family. Beginning

at thirteen, my four siblings and I received special gifts from Mother on a few key birthdays until we turned twenty-one. *Lao Niang*, my grandmother, had practiced this tradition with her children when the family lived in China, where my grandparents served as medical missionaries during Mother's growing up years. After supper tonight, I would get to open my special gifts, and I was anxious to see what they would be.

In Daddy's absence, my grandfather, *Lao E*, sat at the head of the table opposite Mother. I sat to Mother's right. The room was softly lit, and shadows from the fire in the living room fireplace played on the log walls around us and on the beamed ceiling above. The adults engaged in grownup conversation—about my father's work and whereabouts, my grandfather's latest article for *Christianity Today*, and the day's current events—while my siblings and I savored Bea's chicken and teased one another. As usual, our family dinner proved lively and animated, rich in both talk and the occasional shenanigan.

After supper, eyeing my gifts on the sideboard, I sat in my seat eagerly awaiting their presentation. Mother brought my lemon cake with thirteen candles burning like torches over the butter cream icing, and everyone sang "Happy Birthday." As the cake was cut and pieces sent around the table, Mother handed me the stack of gifts. I spotted two gifts that I knew were from her: one a small box and the other just about the size of a book. Everyone's eyes were on me.

In the glow of the fire still blazing in the living room, I opened the gifts, saving the two special gifts from Mother until the end. When I finally got to hers, I chose the one in the small box first. As I unwrapped it, I saw beneath the lid a little bar-pin lined with seed pearls. From the bar, a tiny chain dropped down, and hanging on the chain was a locket. I opened the locket's gold face, inscribed with Mother's initials, to find a teeny picture of my father as a young man on one side and a baby picture of my oldest sister, Gigi, on the other.

Mother explained that her teacher, Miss Lucy Fletcher, an American in China who taught the children of missionaries, had given her the gift on a special occasion. As a girl, Mother had been very close to her teacher, and Miss Fletcher had been a character in our bedtime stories.

Examining the treasure in my hand now, I realized I felt connected to Mother in a new way. She had trusted me with a precious possession, a memento from her beloved China, a token of the happy childhood years that themselves were like treasures in the rich mine of her memory. The photographs inside the locket must have been fitted into place when she was a young wife and mother. I was mesmerized by the gift. Mother had entrusted it to me, and that made me feel special—as if a unique bond now existed between us.

Then I opened Mother's second gift—a book, I expected. Taking off the wrapping paper, I came to a green leather cover decorated only with a border of gold lines. The pages, too, were edged in gold, like the pages of a Bible. But when I opened this book, I saw that the pages were blank. It was a journal.

TAKING OFF THE WRAPPING PAPER, I CAME TO A GREEN LEATHER COVER DECORATED ONLY WITH A BORDER OF GOLD LINES. ...IT WAS A JOURNAL.

Mother was a faithful journal-keeper, and knowing I liked to write too, she was giving me a beautiful, grown-up book in which to record my thoughts and life-events, just like she did. A week after my birthday, Mother suggested I ask an artist friend to inscribe the front page of my new journal in calligraphy. In thick black ink, outlined with light green, our friend emblazoned on the flyleaf a motto that Mother and I knew very well. The words read, "I only count the hours that shine."

"Good-Times" Book

Around the time of my thirteenth birthday, I was absorbed in reading a series of books by a woman named Annie Fellows Johnston, who wrote during the late-nineteenth and early-twentieth centuries. This series chronicled the life of a heroine known as the "Little Colonel," a young girl growing up among the aristocracy of Kentucky.

In one of the books in the series, the Little Colonel—in a moment of despair—is introduced to the practice of journal keeping by her friend Betty. A copious writer, Betty urges her hurting friend to keep a "good-times" book, a journal of happy memories she can reread when she is sad. On the fly-leaf of a blank journal, Betty writes an inscription taken from a sundial—"I only mark the hours that shine"—and gives the book to the Little Colonel to be her very own "good-times" book. [1]

Mother read the Little Colonel books when she was growing up in China, and knowing I loved to read, she had introduced the books to me. Since the books were out of print, Mother helped me write off to second-hand bookstores in order to collect the series. Mother herself was a great book collector and knew how to track down rare and out-of-print volumes. Between Mother and one of her friends, I eventually had the whole series in my possession.

I took readily to the Little Colonel and to her practice of keeping a "good-times" book. Following Mother's encouragement, I tried to fill my new green journal with accounts of happy times—the successes I had sewing my own dresses, the good grades I made in school, and family occasions and events. Mother constantly urged us to go through life accentuating the positive and de-emphasizing the negative, and she seemed to believe my journal keeping would help me to that end.

Once I hit the rocky road of adolescence, sticking to writing only about "shining hours" became a challenge. I went off to boarding school, got very homesick, and struggled to navigate the ins-and-outs of friendship and romance. I was not always able to see the hours that shone, let alone record them. Still, the principle of focusing on good times stuck with me, perhaps because, in addition to encouraging me to keep my chin up, Mother lived out what she taught us: *She* counted the hours that shone, and she worked hard to model an upbeat, positive outlook for my siblings and me.

Mother's Example

Mother is notorious for her dry wit and bright, cheerful approach to life. Blessed with an optimistic spirit, Mother is a great conversationalist and given to laughter and practical jokes. She has her melancholy side, but her spunk and sense of the ridiculous are ever in view. She does not take herself very seriously, and she lovingly chides with a "pooh!" those given to too much seriousness.

THROUGHOUT MY LIFE, MOTHER HAS BROUGHT LIGHT-HEARTEDNESS TO BEAR ON EVEN OUR MOST PROFOUND DISAPPOINTMENTS. FOR AS LONG AS I CAN REMEMBER, SHE HAS REPEATED THE ADAGE, "MAKE THE MOST OF ALL THAT COMES AND THE LEAST OF ALL THAT GOES."

When I was growing up, a familiar sound in our home was the rapid clicking of Mother's heels up and down the hallways. Mother ever seemed to be in the middle of a project, and she had the habit of making the most mundane domestic activities sources of entertainment. On one occasion, Mother and I were grocery shopping and enjoying ourselves so much that another shopper approached us exclaiming she had never seen a mother and daughter having so much fun. Even washing dishes became exciting on Mother's watch. "Let's see how fast we can do them! Let's try to beat the clock!" she would urge.

Mother possesses the uncanny ability to turn just about any situation into an occasion for a joke, and her little pranks are run-of-the-mill at our house on the mountain. Many a visitor given to scanning the beams in the ceilings, for example, has found him or herself startled by little rubber "hedgehogs"— teeny figures with wild hair and wild eyes—grinning from numerous of the knotholes. In all cases, at least those I know about, the perpetrator who positioned the absurd-looking hedgehogs was none other than Mother.

Mother has been known to leave a sheen of mirth on more alarming states-of-affairs, too. One afternoon some years ago, she was driving a friend—who had just lost her son and needed cheering—up the steep ascent to our house. When Mother got to the top of the driveway, she mistakenly hit the accelerator instead of the brake and went sailing over the mountain! By the time others arrived at the scene, the two elderly ladies, thankfully unscathed, were both in stitches with laughter and Mother's friend sufficiently cheered. After the incident, Mother arranged for a stop sign to be staked down in the ravine lest other drivers consider pursuing her newly pioneered detour!

Throughout my life, Mother has brought lightheartedness to bear on even our most profound disappointments. For as long as I can remember, she has repeated the adage, "Make the most of all that comes and the least of all that goes." Mother would remind us of this principle when we were homesick at boarding school, suffering from an embarrassing experience, or feeling remorseful over a bad grade. She explained that seeing the sunny side of life—and letting bygones be bygones—was a choice, and one she wanted us to learn to make for ourselves. The alternative—camping in sorrow—she portrayed as destructive, unpleasant, and, ultimately, self-defeating.

And yet, for all of her good cheer and vivacity, Mother deeply understands the pain, ugliness, and suffering of life. She is not in denial; she does not gloss over sorrow or try to ignore it. Her whimsical nature is well balanced with compassion and sensitivity, both of which she has offered me in abundance during periods of my life when I have experienced loss and heartache. In fact, Mother's knowledge of pain may be what has produced the depth of her joy. She can count the hours that shine because she has been privy to some pretty dim hours, and those from a very young age.

SHE EXPLAINED THAT SEEING THE SUNNY SIDE OF LIFE—AND LETTING BYGONES BE BYGONES—WAS A CHOICE, AND ONE SHE WANTED US TO LEARN TO MAKE FOR OUR-SELVES.

Pain and Joy

Mother grew up in a bandit-ridden China where horrible fates befell people daily, and citizens lived in fear that crime would darken their doorsteps at any moment. People were routinely kidnapped, for example, and sometimes dismembered, to extract ransom from relatives. One missionary, whom Mother knew, was captured by bandits and then gunned down in cold blood.

In keeping with a grisly cultural practice, infants who died or who were close to death, often were left out of doors in Mother's town and exposed to the elements. Mother helped rescue at least one of these babies. I have heard differing accounts as to whether the infant survived, but regardless, the experience made a very strong impression on Mother, who was then just a girl.

Mother's surroundings in China were never secure. She has often told us of being able to see bombs in the berths of Japanese fighter planes flying overhead during Japan's invasion of China. When Mother left the country for Wheaton College in America, as she writes in her book, *It's My Turn*, she was forced to depart on a U.S. troopship evacuating naval families from an alternative port, because the Japanese had mined the

Yangtze river and blown up the Nanking-Shanghai rail line (Revell, 1982). [2]

The chaos comprising the backdrop of Mother's formative years no doubt touched her child's heart in a profound way. From an early age, Mother developed a deep relationship with God, suggesting her heart was soft and tender—and vulnerable to pain. And yet despite the suffering she witnessed while growing up, Mother repeatedly says that she did not "know fear," and that she felt secure in China. Even now, Mother constantly refers to her "happy childhood" and "happy memories" and the fun of her early years in a treacherous country.

How does Mother explain this happiness? Quite simply, Mother attributes her joy and upbeat perspective to her parents' example. Whatever dangers were outside the walls of their home, Mother says, *Lao E* and *Lao Niang* did not show signs of being worried or afraid. My grandparents were not putting on an act in front of their children. They prayed, trusted God, and exercised faith in him by deliberately practicing joy. They *chose* not to be afraid. *Lao E*, whom Mother adored, would come home at night after his rounds at the local hospital—where he was head of surgical work and where he most certainly witnessed the grim realities of life in China at that time—and he would preside over family gath-

FROM HER PARENTS' EXAMPLE, SHE LEARNED THAT PAIN DID NOT HAVE TO WEAKEN OR SQUELCH ONE'S JOY. PAIN AND JOY COULD COEXIST.

erings with his wife and children, holding hymn-sings around the piano, playing games like Rook and Parcheesi, and reading the classics aloud.

Lao Niang, too, created a festive, fanciful atmosphere for the family. Once during a birthday celebration, she placed a pan of water in the center of the dinner table so a little clique of baby ducklings could paddle back and forth while everyone ate. As family lore has it, when it came time to sing "Happy Birthday," the ducklings swam to the end of the pan where the birthday girl sat and opened and closed their bills as if they, too, were singing.

Mother saw life's cold realities during her years in China—and she saw her parents' response to those realities. From her parents' example, she learned that pain did not have to weaken or squelch one's joy. Pain and joy could coexist. To quote one of her poems, Mother learned to "live with pain" and enjoy life at the same time. Thus, when she became an adult, making "the most of all that comes and the least of all that goes" became a lifestyle Mother readily embraced. While she certainly has wrestled with her own suffering, heartache, and disappointment over the years—giving her great depth of faith and compassion for others—Mother has spent a lifetime cultivating joy. And for that she is incredibly resilient.

We live a time
secure;
beloved and loving,
sure
it cannot last
for long
then—
the good-byes come
again—again—
like a small death,
the closing of a door.
One learns to live
with pain.
One looks ahead,
not back—
never back,
only before.
And joy will come again—
warm and secure,
if only for the now,
laughing,
we endure.

—Ruth Bell Graham / *Collected Poems*, 185

Mother's Writing

Throughout her life, one of Mother's great loves has been writing. In writing, Mother had an outlet for both joy and pain. She worked out her emotions as she wrote; she communicated with God, let her imagination roam, and developed her thoughts. To the blank page she could bring her struggles and issues, her gratitude and whimsy.

Perhaps the best description of Mother's motivation for writing can be found in the introduction to her *Collected Poems*. Referencing an explanation printed in an earlier volume of her poems, Mother wrote, "[T]hese poems were never written for publication. Primarily, I wrote them for myself. I've written because, at times, I had to. It was write, or develop an ulcer. I chose to write. At times I wrote for sheer fun." [3]

Better than anything else, I believe, it is Mother's poetry that reflects who she is most completely. In Mother's poetry, one can perceive her winsomeness and her melancholy; her passion for God and her sense of inadequacy before him; her faith and her fear;

her dependence on God; her hunger for wisdom; and her need for the comfort of the heavenly Father. One senses the balance and depth of Mother in the range of her work.

Throughout our growing up years, Mother kept journals and notebooks full of poems. She routinely kept a small notebook in her purse and seemed ever to be writing down quotations she liked, sermon notes, good ideas, and witticisms. Frequently, she would share with us some of the fun little poems and ditties she had written down in spare moments, or adages, of which she seemed to have a never-ending supply.

Aside from her frequent note-taking, however, we did not often *see* Mother in the act of composing or journaling; mostly, she wrote of her deepest thoughts and feelings when she was alone. To us, perhaps the most obvious testament of Mother's passion for writing was her desk—although, I should probably say her passion for writing *and studying*, for Mother's writing and studying go hand-in-hand.

A great reader, Mother always seemed to be delving simultaneously into a wide variety of books. Among those might be a current best-seller, a biography, and various spiritual books. If Mother needed comfort, she might reach for one kind of book; if she needed to laugh, she might reach for another; and again, if she was looking for intellectual stimulation, she might reach for yet another. When asked once why she did not finish one book before beginning another, she replied, "One does not finish all of the pickles before opening the olives."

Whatever books Mother was reading could be found in stacks beside her bed—and, most certainly, on her desk. Entering Mother's room from the bright hallway, you do not notice her desk at first. You must turn around and face the doorway to see it—not simply a desk, but a whole study area. During my growing-up years, as I recall, Mother's desk was a door set atop two filing cabinets. Later she studied at a wooden table positioned between a tall chest of drawers and another desk topped with a ceiling-high set of shelves. Her desk evolved over the years to suit her needs and according to what pieces of furniture were available.

We children only went to the desk at Mother's bidding or with permission. We understood this to be her personal, private area, and we knew to treat her desk with respect. Mother's desk was a world unto itself. I was fascinated by it—and still am! The desk was loaded with resource books—any number of versions of the Scripture, Bible commentaries, and other sundry reference materials. I particularly remember a set of John Trapp's Bible commentaries, leather-bound books she found in England and to which she frequently referred. Mother's notebooks were stacked on her desk, too, alongside a big mug of writing utensils, which included the

Rapidograph pen she used to make notations on the India paper in her Bible.

On the wall in front of her desk, Mother hung a crown of thorns, which a Muslim policeman made for her in 1960 when she was walking down the Mount of Olives near Jerusalem; and two crosses made of sticks by my brother Franklin and a playmate when they were boys. Photographs of dear ones also hung on the wall; and above the crown of thorns hung a plaque displaying an adage, "Fear not tomorrow, God is already there."

But perhaps the most distinctive and constant feature of Mother's desk was her open Bible. She kept it front and center on the desk and would read from it throughout the day, taking a few moments here and there to glean nuggets of truth. Other books and notebooks might stay open alongside Mother's Bible, showing the desk as a place in constant use. And her desk *was* in constant use. For in Mother's case, Bible reading, studying, writing, and learning were not so much activities as states of being.

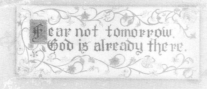

Seeing the Light

Mother gave me little diaries from the time I was very young. In them I faithfully recorded what I believed were the basics of every day: what my siblings and I did, and what time I went to bed. A stickler for order and routine, I allotted a page per day, and all the entries were almost exactly the same number of lines of carefully printed letters.

When I was eleven, Mother gave me a little red journal to take with me on a trip I was making to the other side of the world with *Lao E* and *Lao Niang*. My grandparents had worked in China for nearly twenty-five years, and now my grandfather served on the Board of World Missions for what was the Presbyterian Church in the United States denomination—also called the Southern Presbyterian Church. He and my grandmother were slated to make a tour of missions works in Korea, where their daughter, my Aunt Virginia, served as a missionary with her husband. I was invited to come along.

I loved every minute of this special trip with my grandparents—I was their guest and had them all to myself. We traveled to Asia by way of Alaska, where we spent a day touring the glaciers and waterways. Once we arrived in Korea, we stayed in Seoul with my aunt and uncle and also journeyed to rural areas of the country. We experienced the markets and daily living. I loved the exotic smells and the people's dress. On the way home, we traveled by way of Hawaii where I was able to visit my great-uncle's grave at the National Memorial Cemetery of the Pacific at Punchbowl. All along, I tried to record my experiences and observations, as Mother had instructed me, so I would not forget what I had seen.

For as long as I can remember, I have wanted to write. When I was a young adult, as I recall, the editor of *Decision Magazine* told me the best way to learn to write was to read widely. I tried to do so, following Mother's lead. With her encouragement, I tried my hand at poetry too, especially during my courtship and early-married years, perhaps having in mind some of Mother's early love poems about Daddy.

I also maintained the discipline of chronicling my life's events. Much later, when I traveled to China with my mother and two sisters, Anne and Gigi, in 1989, I was assigned the role of "scribe" for the trip. By then I was nearly forty years old and still known among loved ones as the journal keeper!

But I have found that writing—particularly journaling— is much more than chronicling events. As I imagine must be true for Mother, writing helps me clarify my thinking and get perspective on life. I do record events, but then I try to apply Scripture to those events. I ask God to reveal himself to me in the details of my circumstances as I write them out, and I listen for his voice. I may come to my journal with a jumble of disconnected facts and perceptions; but once I am finished writing, I often have a much better understanding of both what has happened and what perspective I need to adopt.

In this respect, journaling is a true means of encouragement, which is what the Little Colonel's "good-times" book was meant to be after all. Even as the Little Colonel went back and reread her happy entries, I like to go back to my journals and see what I was dealing with at different times in life, where significant growth took place, and how God answered my prayers.

Not all of the hours I count in my journal are what might be called shining hours. I have suffered losses, made wrong decisions, and experienced pain. I have used writing as a way to make sense of these hurts. Writing has been an act of wrestling for me—wrestling to achieve the balanced, upbeat perspective that my mother has modeled; wrestling to keep hold of joy in the midst of heartache; wrestling to understand God's view of my struggles and to maintain hope.

And yet, aren't these instances of struggle also shining hours? For in my record of them, I see not so much my own darkness as the bright light of the One upholding me in the midst of the struggle—the One whose light, the Bible says, darkness cannot overcome (John 1:5, NRSV). Perhaps this is the key to counting the hours that shine: understanding that what makes the hours shine is not the absence of hardship—what we would call darkness—but the presence of the Light.

From this perspective, in fact, all hours could be counted as shining hours. For there is no place we can go where the light of God will not shine. David wrote, "Where can I go from Your Spirit? Or where can I flee from Your presence?" (Psalm 139:7) An awareness of God's constant presence must be Mother's secret, I think. She sees the bright side of life because she walks with the Savior—the "Light of the world" (John 8:12). She communes with the One to whom, as Scripture says, "the night is as bright as the day" (Psalm 139:12).

THE GROWING DARKNESS CLOSES IN
LIKE SOME THICK FOG,
ENGULFING ME—
A CREEPING HORROR—
TILL I LEARNED,
"THE DARKNESS HIDETH NOT
FROM THEE."

—Ruth Bell Graham / *Collected Poems*, 84

CHAPTER 2

'54

ℒIVING THROUGH HOMESICKNESS

From thy brier shall blow a rose for others.
AMY CARMICHAEL

IT WAS AUTUMN, though I would not have known it by my surroundings. I was thirteen years old, just a month or two into my first year at boarding school in Central Florida, and desperately missing Little Piney Cove, which is what we call our home on the mountain in Montreat, North Carolina. I missed the familiar autumn smells: dried leaves on the forest floor, smoke from the fireplaces. I missed the mountains and the low, afternoon light this time of year. I missed Mother and

Daddy, my grandparents and my siblings. I missed the season's brilliant reds and oranges that from our mountain vista seemed to go on for miles and miles.

Nothing around me in Florida brought comfort. None of the faces. None of the scenery. It was a painful distance between this place and home. And I ached.

After lunch ended on this particular day, I walked from the dining hall to what we called the "Cow Palace," a student gathering place, to buy some candy and pick up my mail before class. The school was situated on a beautiful estate, but I hardly noticed now as I walked. My thoughts were else-where—I was fighting back tears.

Once I got to my mailbox, my spirits lifted instantly. On the outside of one of the envelopes I spotted Mother's distinctive, leftward-sloping handwriting in thick black ink. Turning the letter over in my hands, I saw the comforting print of our return address: "Little Piney Cove."

Quickly collecting my things, I started off to the building where my Algebra class was supposed to meet at the next bell. I got to the room, set my books on a desk and tore into the envelope, pulling out the several pages of neatly folded sta-tionary. Then I took my seat and began to read.

Mother's letters were always newsy and descriptive; they made me feel I was back at home, included in everything, missed and talked of and prayed for regularly by family members. Mother had a knack for keeping her five children together in mind and spirit. She sent news to us of one another with such frequency that we still felt a part of one another's daily lives, though we were scattered around the world.

As I sat reading now in the Florida classroom, I found this day's letter did not bring the comfort and assurance of belonging for which I had hoped. Perhaps I was already so melancholy when I came to the letter that no words could have soothed or cheered me. In fact,  Mother's handwriting and her news only caused me to miss home with more passion than before.

Tears ran down my face as I read the detailed narrative—this one about my older sister Anne's horse, Chevy, who had foaled while I was away. Scenes came to mind from all the afternoons Anne and I had spent horseback riding together after school. Mr. Rickman, one of my parents' helpers, would have picked us up from school in the Jeep and driven us to the stables, and then afterward taken us back up the mountain for supper. Anne and I would have been tired from the exercise and fresh air—ready to eat and to see Mother, and Daddy, if he were home.

Suddenly, the sound of footsteps outside the classroom

startled me from my daydream. Looking up from Mother's letter, I saw an upperclassman come breezing in; he was cutting through our classroom to get to his own. I tried to smile as he threw me a friendly look, but my tears betrayed me.

"What's wrong?" he asked in a tone of concern.

I looked down and then stammered, "I'm . . . I'm homesick." There. I had admitted it. What else could I say? I couldn't pretend.

"Oh," he said kindly. "Don't worry. It will get better. It really will."

I could not imagine that happening, but I smiled through the tears, wiped my cheeks, and turned my gaze back to the letter. In the envelope, Mother had included a little red notebook, which she instructed me to use for note taking during chapel talks. I was to fill the book with "choice tidbits" and "potent phrases," she explained—whatever stuck in my mind and made me think. I thought of her little notebooks tucked into

The tear-stained letter

her purse and filled up with just such tidbits and phrases; and as I read her words to me, tears continued to roll down my cheeks and hit the paper, smearing the ink.

When I got to the end of the letter, I saw that Mother had anticipated me: it was almost as if she were there in the room, aware of my tears and ready to encourage. She urged me to "gather up all the good and beautiful and worthwhile" aspects of my experience at the school—as always, teaching me to see the best in my circumstances and look on the bright side. In fact, she seemed to have known I would be feeling defeated and lonesome, for, true to form, her last word to me was: "SMILE."

I WAS TO FILL THE BOOK WITH "CHOICE TIDBITS" AND "POTENT PHRASES," SHE EXPLAINED—WHATEVER STUCK IN MY MIND AND MADE ME THINK.

Mother's Homesickness

Mother did not take my homesickness lightly. She was not trying to bypass my hurt by insisting I cheer up. Mother was well acquainted with homesickness—she knew how it felt.

Mother has often told the story of her experience leaving home for boarding school at the age of thirteen. Her family lived in what was then called Tsingkiangpu—which today is part of the larger metropolitan area of Huaiyin in Jiangsu Province—north of Shanghai. When it came time for Mother and her older sister, Rosa, to go to a formal school, *Lao E* and *Lao Niang* chose a Christian boarding school for foreign students in what is today Pyongyang, North Korea. To get there, Mother would have to depart from Shanghai and travel by boat to Japan, where she would take a train and then a ferry to get to the Korean peninsula.

On September 2, 1933, my grandparents, along with Lucy Fletcher—Mother's tutor—accompanied Mother, Rosa, and a few other foreign children to Shanghai to prepare for the students' departure. The group overnighted in a missionary boarding house at Number Four Quinsan Gardens where Mother and her family had stayed often during their travels—to America on furlough, for instance.

Now, in the fall of 1933, Mother was spending the night in the familiar Victorian brick building one last time before she left her loved ones for a strange country, about a week's journey away. Lying in bed that evening, desperate to stay behind with her parents, Mother offered a prayer of great significance in the annals of our family history: she asked God to let her die before morning rather than make her embark on the long journey to school in another land.

What strikes me now about this scene is the intensity of Mother's desperation—for someone so young to pray to die! After all, Mother wasn't going to be setting sail alone. She had her sister, Rosa, who had attended the school the year before, and childhood friends along, too. That Mother would rather have died than be forced to make the journey points to the profound attachment she must have felt to her parents and her home. Suffering the presence of bandits, who murdered and kidnapped, apparently was preferable to living somewhere apart from *Lao E* and *Lao Niang*, apart from the secure environment they had created at home in Tsingkiangpu.

Needless to say, God did not grant Mother's petition to die in Shanghai. And as she feared, her introduction to school in Korea

Dormitories at Pyeng Yang Foreign School

Mother and her schoolmates

Permit issued by the local government authorities for Mother to attend school

did prove exceedingly difficult for her. She cried herself to sleep at night. She wrote numerous and lengthy letters home, begging her parents to let her return. She penned one meandering lament on a six-foot-long Japanese scroll!

Lao E and *Lao Niang* remained resolute, though, and for all of her angst, Mother had to stay put. Eventually, her spirits did lift and her homesickness subsided a little, though not without hard work on her part. Mother has called her boarding school experience "boot camp." [1] In the trenches of melancholy, confusion, loneliness, and despair, she gained the emotional and spiritual training she would need for future trials in life. And when her own daughter—her third child—found herself in a similarly despairing position, Mother had plenty of wisdom to dispense.

Mother's Faithfulness

For me, life away from home did get easier, as the young man who passed me in my Algebra classroom had promised; but I struggled with homesickness throughout my years at boarding school. I spent two years at the Florida school and then transferred to another school in New York, where I stayed one year before heading off to Gordon College.

The year in New York was by far the most difficult of my years away from home. By then, I had grown accustomed to the school in Florida with its familiar Christian culture, its Southern gentility and vibrant social life. By contrast, the school in New York offered an intellectual emphasis and more liturgical forms of Christian expression with which I was not then acquainted. I had mononucleosis when I arrived, and a trunk now filled with school uniforms and tie-up shoes in lieu of party dresses. I most definitely felt like a fish out of water.

FROM THE FIRST LETTER SHE WROTE WHEN I WENT OFF TO SCHOOL, MOTHER NEVER CHANGED HER TUNE. SHE ONLY ADDED LINES OF HARMONY.

Through it all, Mother wrote to me with remarkable regularity—she wrote long letters full of encouragement, advice, Scriptures, and, as always, news of home and loved ones. She even wrote me the occasional rebuke! Looking back at my stacks of letters from Mother, I am amazed by the detailed attention she gave my adolescent issues and concerns. She prayed for me faithfully and always had a word of hope or direction to give me out of what she had received from God through prayer.

Mother wrote to me whether she was in the mountains or on the Mediterranean, at our house or the White House. She was faithful in her role as parent and guide, and I was just one of her five children! That Mother would spend such time and energy writing me lengthy letters—especially from places where she could have been interacting with dignitaries—only illustrates the truth about Mother's priorities. She was a wife and mother first. My siblings and I were her responsibility, assigned to her by God, and she was determined to give her all in rearing and directing us.

Mother's Advice

Several pieces of advice crop up again and again in the letters Mother wrote to me during my adolescent years. From the first letter she wrote when I went off to school, Mother never changed her tune. She only added lines of harmony.

Let Homesickness Drive You to God

Mother always encouraged me that through my experiences away from home, my relationship with Jesus would become more real to me, and my Bible a more important part of my life. "I know that in looking back," she once wrote, "the most difficult times in my life have been the most spiritually productive."

The blues, Mother assured me, were part of being human—permitted by God partly to remind me of my need for him. I certainly could take time to grieve and be sad; Mother advised me to find time to have a good cry when I needed it—in my bed at night, for instance. But I was not to wallow in grief. Rather, I was to let my homesickness drive me to God.

"All these experiences," Mother wrote, "however trying, however irritating, will prove invaluable training for the days ahead if you learn . . . the lessons He would teach you—particularly how sufficient He is under every circumstance and how His Word comes to life for us when we are in difficulty."

As Mother continued to share layers of advice in her letters, I came to understand that I would learn all the lessons God wanted to teach me only if I accepted my lot, which could be summed up in a few words: I was not going home. I had to quit resisting, and Mother faithfully provided instruction about how to let go:

"Just say to the Lord, 'I'm all yours. Take [this time]... and use me here…to be a radiant witness for Christ.' Surrender yourself, your right to happiness, personal preferences etc. And accept each day, each girl, each class assignment, each happening, as they come. And accept them as a special gift from Him—an opportunity to learn, to serve Him."

Perhaps this was just the kind of thing *Lao E* and *Lao Niang* wrote to Mother when she was resisting, to no avail, her own "boot camp" experience.

Find Others Who are Homesick and Cheer Them Up

When Mother was homesick in what is now Pyongyang, her father wrote to one of the overseers at the school and suggested Mother needed to get out of her room more often. "We feel Ruth has a slight tendency to revel in the sad side of things," her father wrote, "letting her religion (which is exceedingly real and precious to her) take a slightly morbid turn." [2]

The overseer, Mabel Axworthy, promptly made Mother a "mother" to the eighth-graders; and, apparently, focusing on the needs of these students took Mother's mind off of her own woes and helped her settle down—at least to some degree.

Mother prescribed me a similar antidote during my years away at school, and she prescribed it constantly: I was to find those students who were unhappy like I was and make it my business to cheer them up. *Turn from yourself. Focus on mak-*

ing others happy. Be a good listener. Show interest in others. Ask questions to express interest. Encourage. These were the kinds of things I read in so many of Mother's letters.

"Every girl there [at school] has problems, worries, frustrations, complexes that they try to hide under a normal exterior," she once wrote in typical fashion. "Try to <u>be</u> a friend instead of wishing for one. Make it a point to say something encouraging to everyone with whom you talk."

Don't Gripe—Cultivate Cheerfulness

I must have tended toward complaining while away at school—or perhaps Mother was simply trying to help me discipline my very human response to hardship—because so many of my letters from her contain the admonition: don't gripe!

"Let joking take the place of griping," she instructed after she sent me off to school for the first time. "Remember how *Lao [E]* breaks the tension with a funny comment?"

Mother emphasized the difference

Mother, Age 13

between what she called a "legitimate airing of gripes" and the "habit of griping," which, she warned, could become "contagious and depressing." To avoid slipping into this bad habit, I was to "cultivate cheerfulness."

But how was I to do that? How did one cultivate cheerfulness? Mother never gave me advice without including practical applications, and when it came to cultivating cheerfulness, she took me right back to one of her other key pieces of advice: focus on others.

"Ask the Lord each day how you can help the others. Encourage them, praise them, appreciate them, listen to them, love them."

She also wrote: "Smile when you feel like crying. You'd be surprised how many others feel like crying, too. This world is so full of heart-ache."

Lean on God

Throughout my adolescent years, whether I was struggling with homesickness, boy troubles, or other issues, Mother taught me how to lean on the Lord. Leaning on God, she explained, was the secret to living through homesickness.

Mother both modeled "leaning" and gave me direction so that I could learn how to do it myself. She often applied Scriptures directly to my circumstances, showing me how to make the Bible relevant in my daily life.

"It's just as well to pray and quietly wait," she wrote when I was unsure about how to interact with a boy. "'Fretting,' remember, 'tends only to evil doing' (Psalm 37) such as talking too much, confiding in too many people (and some talk too much too), [and] getting more hot and bothered inside. My advice: Play it cool."

In the same letter, Mother put the responsibility on *me* to lean on God. She asked, "Can you commit this to the Lord? Just roll it all on Him? (Read Ps. 37 again.)"

In fact, during my year in New York, I began leaning on God without any prompting and out of sheer necessity. I was so unhappy that each morning when I heard the rooster crow, my heart filled with dread. I realized perhaps for the first time how badly I needed God, and I began to ask him each day for help. Mother's instructions started to take hold, and just as was her habit at home, I started leaving my Bible open on my desk, so I could come back to it throughout the day and glean nuggets of truth and encouragement.

Illustrating God

Perhaps I was able to absorb Mother's advice because of the way she presented it. Mother maintained a necessary parental distance in our relationship—she spoke firmly as my parent on numerous occasions, correcting and directing me with a mother's unambiguous authority. But she also let me know that she was human like me. She knew what it was like to battle with the griping habit. She knew the sorrow of missing home. She needed the Scriptures and the Lord's guidance just as badly as I did.

SOMETHING ABOUT MOTHER'S STOOPING DOWN IN THIS MOMENT TO RELATE TO ME, HER HURTING CHILD, MADE ME FEEL SIGNIFICANT AND LOVED. I FELT UNDERSTOOD, KNOWN BY MOTHER. AND I FELT I KNEW HER BETTER, TOO.

In one instance, Mother identified with my homesickness on a particularly deep level. She had just put me on a plane after Christmas break to send me back to school in New York. I did not want to go; I wanted to stay at Little Piney Cove. But Mother took me to the airport as planned and sat in the car watching while my plane took off. When she got home, she wrote me a letter. In the letter, Mother explained that she had only been able to let me go because she knew God was going back to school with me. Then she shared a memory:

> Oddly enough, as I think of you there, someone on the T.V. in Daddy's room is playing "The Swallow." I was a little younger than you and was on the train going from Fusan (now Pusan), Korea up to PyengYang. We had an old record player and that was one of the records. I played it over and over, the beauty and poignancy of it

somehow relieving the ache inside me. I never hear it now that I am not carried back to that moment—the lurching train, the old 3rd class car clackety-clacking over the rails, one lonely, empty kid and that beautiful song. And tonight it is played again.

Something about Mother's stooping down in this moment to relate to me, her hurting child, made me feel significant and loved. I felt understood, known by Mother. And I felt I knew her better, too. She had let me glimpse her heart. Not just in this letter, but often. She communicated with me in so many different tones, and frequently all in one letter. She brought news, gave advice, provided insight, encouraged, cheered, chastised, loved, and joked. I saw many sides of Mother. She let those different sides show. She trusted me, and I trusted her. We loved each other. We had a relationship.

What strikes me now is that in the many ways Mother built our relationship, she illustrated the way God deals with us as children. God knows and loves us completely. As was true of Mother, God loves us when he corrects us. He applies discipline and then lets us know how proud he is of us. He tells us what is on his mind and shows us what to do. He stoops down to relate to us. He understands what we go through. He grieves when we grieve and rejoices when we rejoice. He keeps confidences. He is completely trustworthy. He cheers us on.

It is because I have a relationship with God that I am able to receive his instruction, encouragement, and discipline. I know that I am significant to him. I know that he loves me, that I am special to him. I know that when God corrects me, he is doing so for good reason. Certainly, I have struggled— and questioned God during trial and difficulty. There have been times when, not trusting God, I have run ahead in my own understanding and made mistakes. In dark moments, I have wondered if God cared about me at all. Ultimately, however, I do trust God—I have *learned* to trust him. And Mother has helped me to that end. Loving me as she does, she has shown me what it means to be God's child, and that has made all the difference.

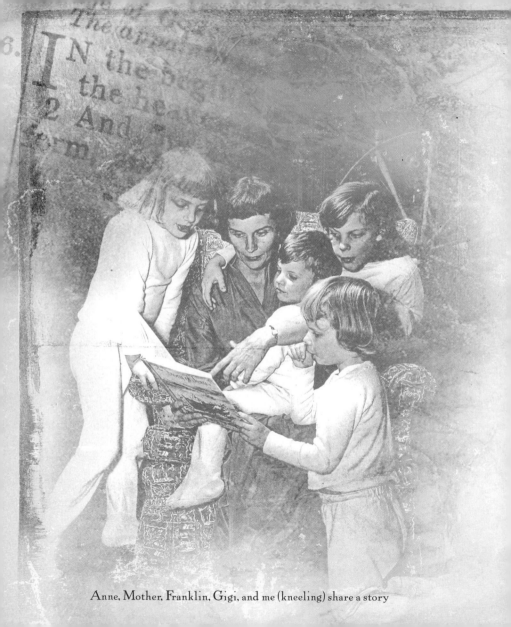

Anne, Mother, Franklin, Gigi, and me (kneeling) share a story

CHAPTER 3

ℒOVING GOD

Abiding is not hanging on but dwelling in.

W. GRAHAM SCROGGIE

MOTHER HAD ALREADY tucked me in, but I could not sleep for the night noises. The crickets' song pulsated beneath my window, and I thought I could hear twigs crackling and wings fluttering. I opened my eyes and kept watch. Some nights previous, a bat had flown through my open window while I was sleeping, and now I feared the same thing might happen again. I pulled the covers, an armor of quilts, tightly around me.

Within moments, I was out of bed, padding down the hall-way to the back staircase. The covers weren't helping—I wanted to talk to Mother. If I could just tell her that I was scared, then she would reassure me; she would tell me what to do. I descended the staircase quietly, and nearing the bottom, I saw a glow of light in the hallway coming from Mother's room. Her door, just beside the staircase, was open, and I felt relieved as I approached.

Putting my hand on the doorframe, I peered into the dim room, trying not to make any noise. A fire was burning in the fireplace, and shadows danced across the braided rugs that covered the dark wood floor. Mother was kneeling at her bedside. Her back was turned to me. Her head was bowed. Nearby on the bed, I saw her open Bible, but she was not reading. She was praying.

FAITH WAS THE VERY HEARTBEAT OF LIFE AT LITTLE PINEY COVE. WE BEGAN AND ENDED EACH DAY AS A FAMILY ON OUR KNEES IN PRAYER.

I paused in the doorway to see if Mother would stir. Had she heard me? I waited and watched, taking in the features of the room: the blue-and-white tiles that made a border around the fireplace; the big bay window, dark now and giving back the room's reflection; the pile of books beside Mother's bed, overshadowed by a blue-and-white half-canopy; and finally, Mother again, in her gown, kneeling.

Mother did not move, and I did not want to disturb her. I knew that if I waited for her to finish praying, I would be waiting for a long time. Looking at Mother kneeling beside her comfortable bed, loaded with pillows and blankets, my limbs began to grow heavy, and I wished I could lie down. I realized there was only one thing to do. Turning away from Mother, the open Bible, the fire, and the room, I went back to the staircase and began to climb.

Everyday Faith

Faith was the very heartbeat of life at Little Piney Cove. We began and ended each day as a family on our knees in prayer. One of my earliest memories is of kneeling down beside the fireplace at our first home—called the Old House—and fiddling with a loose brick on the hearth during family devotions.

Of course, my father's work meant the activities of faith were uppermost in the minds of the adults in our midst. We constantly received reports about my father's evangelistic meetings; and when we were young, Mother would set up a globe in the kitchen and show us where Daddy was preaching at any given time. Every Sunday afternoon at three o'clock we gathered around the radio in the living room to listen to my father's weekly broadcast, "The Hour of Decision." When Daddy came home from his travels, we often knew he had arrived by the cables running from the driveway into the house—a sign to us as we got home from school that he was in his office taping "The Hour of Decision."

But while my father, due to his demanding schedule, lived out faith for us largely from afar—and he loved us very dearly—Mother lived out her faith in front of us day in and day out. She was more often our primary example.

Mother, Franklin, Gigi, Anne, Daddy, and me (on Daddy's lap)

Mother's was a practical, everyday faith. Her faith touched all that she did, but not in an ostentatious kind of way. Mother expressed her faith and her love of God through the common activities of life. Her conversation, for example, was suffused with talk of what God was teaching her. We constantly overheard her discussing the Scriptures with adults or sharing stories of people she knew whose lives had been changed by God through Christ. Her countenance softened—

and it still does—when she talked about God.

Mother also seemed to draw countless spiritual lessons from ordinary activities, and she shared those lessons with us. Hiking up the ridge with us in the afternoons, she might point out a particular tree or bird or view of the mountains and then use what she saw to help us understand a biblical principle or a character trait of God. Things like arguments among us children and dilemmas we faced at school likewise afforded Mother material for spiritual illustrations. In fact, it seemed she could use just about anything to teach us a truth.

For example: I remember a time when the main road into the nearby city of Asheville was being resurfaced. Lines had not yet been painted onto the road, and Mother would reference the bare black top to make the point that in life, people needed guidelines. Without guidelines, she explained, people became insecure and could end up driving in the wrong lane and causing accidents. She meant her point to be both literal and figurative, of course; and, ultimately, we understood what kind of "guidelines" she had in mind—biblical ones.

More recently, Mother was sitting with a visitor and me looking out at the patch of lawn in the front of our house and the few sentinel pine trees growing up above the lawn from lower ground. Mother told us that, originally, she and my father had planned to build our home at a lower spot on the mountain, about where those three pine trees were standing. In order for the house to have a view, Mother and Daddy would have had to cut those trees down. Daddy was open to doing so, but Mother was not. Apparently, the property's original homesteader had carried the trees as saplings on his back all the way from Mount Mitchell, the highest point east of the Mississippi. Mother could not bear to fell the trees after such a sacrifice.

To solve the problem, Mother explained, she and Daddy simply decided to build the house at a higher point on the mountain. "I find that to be a good way of solving problems," she said to us, without batting an eye. "Just move to higher ground."

It was as if she had pulled a new adage out of thin air!

Such matter-of-fact, didactic moments punctuated our growing up years with unbelievable frequency. Mother extrapolated little lessons from life easily and naturally. She could see God and his principles in the ordinary, the everyday—perhaps because God and his principles were always on her mind.

But Mother did not just talk about God and his principles; she lived by the principles Christ taught—and lived by them daily. I saw no discrepancy between what she said and what she did, and this consistency is part of what made Mother's relationship with God so powerful to me.

Mother regularly reached out to people in our community who were suffering, and she kept her eyes open for those in need. An alcoholic woman who needed a place to regroup stayed with us in our home. At Christmastime, we delivered baskets to the less fortunate that were packed with gifts and food from the bounty sent to us by friends and supporters. Money given to us by others went into a "help fund," which we would use to meet the small-scale needs of local people. And I would be hard pressed to recall a Sunday dinner that did not include guests from the community whom Mother had invited.

Numerous examples of Mother's goodness to others could be recited here—she made giving a lifestyle; she made it part of what we did as a family. Giving was also an ordinary way of serving God that we children could understand and appreciate. Mother never construed doing for others as a duty or an

The Sentinel Pines

obligation. She loved serving people because she loved God. Serving others was a privilege in her eyes. I remember her saying once, as she offered hospitality to some missionaries in our community, that she was entertaining "God's royalty."

Personal Devotion

Mother's sincere, personal devotion to Christ was something we witnessed on a regular basis. Coming across Mother on her knees praying was not an uncommon experience. We understood from Mother that prayer was personal and vital, not to be treated casually; and when we saw her talking to God in prayer, we did not want to interrupt. We knew that whatever she was talking to him about was important.

Being in the public eye as she was, Mother no doubt kept her deepest feelings to herself. She was extremely private. I remember her telling me once that with regard to her journals, she did not write anything that she thought might embarrass or hurt another person. I suppose Mother understood that her journals were not only for her, but also for posterity, meaning that even her writing could not be a completely safe outlet for her deepest emotions.

Rather, it was Mother's prayer life that afforded her a true channel for her most private thoughts and feelings. Mother, as I have written, strived to make the most of all that came and the least of all that passed her by, but I imagine she must have wrestled with some burdens that were hard to let go, burdens about which no one else knew. With these private issues, Mother went to God. She worked out her struggles on her knees; God was her safe place. As a result, Mother's relationship with God was, and is, very intimate. God truly is her confidant, friend, husband, and father—he is her everything. When, as a young married woman, I went to Daddy for some advice on being a wife, he told me that Mother's secret was "being married to Christ first."

Outside of prayer, Mother expressed her personal devotion to God in other ways that we children could witness. At night after we had gone to bed, for instance, I would hear Mother playing hymns on the piano—one of her favorites was "Come Ye Sinners." She wrote poetry, of course; and she painted beautiful pictures, illustrating spiritual truths. One painting I especially love depicts a large hand protecting sheep from slavering wolves. Mother copied the picture from the jacket of a book called *The Restraining Hand*, published in 1936 and written by a missionary named Rudolf Alfred Bosshardt, who was taken captive by the Red Army in China (Hodder & Stoughton).

Mother's painting, done in what appears to be ink and watercolor, portrays a large hand against the backdrop of a

dark forest. Behind the hand are the wolves, gnashing their teeth; and in front of the hand are the sheep—one reclining, another looking up at the hand with a peaceful expression. To me, the painting illustrates God's promise to protect us. He does not prevent the wolves from coming on the scene, but he does keep them from tearing us apart. When I look at the painting, I gain confidence in God's protection operating in my own life. I think: God is here. I have nothing to fear. I can safely put my trust in him.

To the extent that Mother let us share in her devotional life, she did so partly because she wanted us to learn how to develop our own personal relationships with God. Actually, everything Mother taught us could be said to have equipped us for loving God—whether she was giving us spiritual instruction while on a hike or disciplining us for fighting with one another. (We were a scrappy bunch!) But Mother was also careful to impart specific devotional disciplines to us, and central among these, along with prayer, was the study of Scripture.

Since I can remember, Mother's Bible has been worn and heavily marked, evidence of her passionate devotion to studying God's Word. In fact, over the course of her life, Mother has maintained an almost insatiable desire to learn the truths of the Bible. The Scriptures are part of her warp and woof—they are part of who she is—and from the time we were little she encouraged us, too, in a desire to absorb the Bible's teachings.

In a letter she wrote to me while I was working in Israel the summer before I got married, Mother urged me to take every opportunity to study the Holy Land, because that knowledge would open my eyes to the Scriptures in new ways. She wrote, "Get *The New Israel Atlas* . . . and a good guide book . . . and stuff yourself. I never had enough time for all there is to see and read and learn. The Bible literally comes to life."

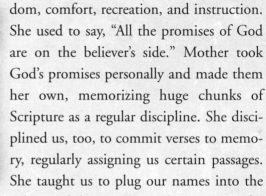

We saw Mother go to her Bible at all times of day for wisdom, comfort, recreation, and instruction. She used to say, "All the promises of God are on the believer's side." Mother took God's promises personally and made them her own, memorizing huge chunks of Scripture as a regular discipline. She disciplined us, too, to commit verses to memory, regularly assigning us certain passages. She taught us to plug our names into the verses, so that we understood them as having been written for us. And we were to read the Scriptures daily, preferably in the morning, so we could enter the day's activities with a bit of truth to chew on and apply as occasions arose.

Mother also gave us copies of books that influenced her own devotional life. She particularly drew inspiration from author and poet Amy Carmichael, the renowned Irish missionary to India, and has given me many of her books over the years. Mother gave each of us a copy of the classic devotional *Streams in the Desert*, which she read regularly. Copies of other devotionals like *Daily Light on the Daily Path* and *Joy and Strength* came to me from Mother, too. (Actually, my one- and six-year-old brothers gave me *Daily Light* one birthday, but Ned and Franklin, of course, were Mother's proxies!)

In all, Mother has set such a beautiful example of a person whose whole purpose is the Lord Jesus. Over her lifetime, she has exerted herself relentlessly to stay connected to God. She prayed and stayed in the Scriptures during both good times and bad. She made the choice daily to look to God as her first love. She modeled persistent—and consistent—faith, and by doing so created for her children a picture of the truly committed life.

Mother is not perfect and never pretended to be. She struggled. She wrestled with God. She labored to make sense of the complexities of life. I am sure she must feel that in some ways she has fallen short. And yet, whether she was on her knees, at her desk, or out with us on the mountain, we children saw her earnestly and determinedly pursuing God, and an understanding of his ways, in everything she undertook.

To me, it is this example of Mother's perseverance and passion—not "perfection"—that stands out. When I struggle in my own life, I think about Mother's love for God, her determination to believe his promises, and her unwavering desire to please him; and I gain strength and inspiration to stay the course. The Bible instructs us to "run with endurance the race that is set before us, fixing our eyes on Jesus" (Hebrews 12:1-2). This is what Mother has done for as long as I have known her. And for her efforts, her sacrifices, her love for her Savior, and her example of personal devotion, I am profoundly grateful.

If I lived within the sound
of the sea's relentless yearning,
my soul would rise and fly to seek
what the soul longs for—unable to speak;
aware, as I go, of Him everywhere:
in my heart, in the clouds . . . in the cold wet air . . .
And my soul would worship in joyful prayer,
receding as the waves recede,
returning with the waves' returning,
reaching up, as for Him, feeling,
then with the waves kneeling . . .
                              kneeling . . .
                                   kneeling . . .

—Ruth Bell Graham / *Collected Poems*, 223

Levity

For all of her spiritual depth and introspection, Mother also made having a relationship with God look desirable. She wasn't morose about faith. Nor was she self-righteous. Mother added levity to godliness, and that made faith attractive. We saw her joy touch all areas of her life. We grew up around happy Christians. Mother often said, "That which is made to be a burden will be shed with relief." I do not know if she was talking about faith, but she certainly made faith seem pleasurable. If we had perceived faith as doom-and-gloom and trying to measure up all the time, then we would have shed it quickly.

Mother used to say this specifically about Bible reading: "If children see you eating your vegetables, then they will learn to like vegetables." By that logic, she assumed that if we saw her reading and enjoying her Bible, then we would excitedly

take on the same discipline. And we did—not all of us right away, but eventually!

Mother, in fact, made the Bible a source of our entertainment. Bible games were staple activities in our home, particularly on Sundays. Television viewing and newspaper reading were off-limits on the Sabbath; Mother and Daddy set Sundays apart for church-going and doing for others. But fun was not off-limits, and on Sunday nights, we children would gather together with my parents and grandparents, and we would play Bible games we called "Spit in the Ocean" and "Twenty Questions." The adults encouraged us in our attempts and laughed with us. *Lao Niang* would let me sit close to her so she could help me as we played. I had so much fun I can even remember one of the bits of trivia I learned in those days: the identity of Maher-shalal-hash-baz—Isaiah's son (Isaiah 8:3).

Levity, of course, was part of Mother's makeup. She was always game for adventure when it came to rearing us, and as I have written, she regularly wove faith lessons into our encounters. As any observer in our home would quickly come to realize, those lessons might emerge out of our zanier foibles and encounters. Here is just the kind of story from which I can imagine Mother extrapolating one of her many spiritual applications.

One summer, Daddy was holding meetings in Europe; and my mother, siblings, and I joined him in Switzerland for several weeks. A host family rented us a house affording a spectacular view of Lake Geneva with the Dents-du-Midi mountain group in the distance. From my nine-year-old perspective, the summer promised to be a dream come true.

Throughout our sojourn, Mother talked with us, as she so often did, about activities that she and her siblings pursued when they were growing up in China. This particular summer, Mother zeroed in on one such activity: sliding down a zip line. Our eyes widened as Mother described a cable stretching down from an upper-story porch to a point on the ground. In China, we learned, the children would stand on the porch, grab onto a pipe attached to the cable, and then descend down the line to ground level, presumably at a rapid rate. My siblings and I were instantly sold on the idea.

In an effort to recreate the zip line in our European environs, Mother collected some rope and a piece of something like piping—maybe a tube—to attach to the rope as a sliding mechanism. We strung the rope from a second-story balcony across the patio and gravel driveway to the lawn. The rope covered a pretty good distance, and sliding down looked like it would be great fun.

As it turned out, I was the brave one to take the first plunge. I grabbed hold of the tube and then stepped off the balcony. And right away, I knew something was amiss. The rope was not taut enough to hold my weight, nor was it smooth for sliding. The tube kept getting caught on the rope and, eventually, sliced my finger. At the first sign of sharp, unexpected pain, I let go of the tube, falling to the ground— actually, to the gravel. I was not hurt by the fall, but we were all disappointed. So much for that adventure!

Remembering the scene now, I can almost hear Mother identifying a spiritual lesson in the ordeal. After tending to me, she might have smiled and said (or thought) something like: *Well, at least we now know to be careful about what we hold on to—if it isn't dependable, we might fall!*

If You Love Me

Jesus said, "'He who has My commandments and keeps them is the one who loves Me" (John 14:21). One of the most striking things in my view about Mother's spiritual life has been her attitude of obedience to God. If Mother believes the Lord is directing her to do something, then there is no question as to whether she will do it. Whereas I may argue, struggle, and wrestle with God, saying, "I don't know if I should do this," Mother seems to yield immediately. Her attitude is, and has been since I can remember, "My Commander has spoken; it is my joy to follow." Her obedience to God is the real proof of her love for him.

When I was a young married woman, Mother wrote me a letter outlining some of the principles she was learning as she studied the book of Exodus.

> I THINK WHEN A CHILD OF GOD IS IN DIFFICULT OR DESPERATE STRAITS HE WOULD DO WELL TO STUDY EX. 5 & 6 CAREFULLY. HOW OFTEN THE PROMISE OF REDEMPTION IS FOLLOWED BY A WORSENING OF THE SITUATION. (CHAP. 5) YET GOD MULTIPLIES DIFFICULTIES TO DEMONSTRATE HIS POWER. AT SUCH TIMES HIS GREATEST ASSURANCE TO US IS, 'I AM THE LORD' (6:2, 8, 29). WE SHOULD FEED OUR SOULS AND FORTIFY OUR HEARTS ON THAT. THEN GO AND DO WHAT HE COMMANDS. WHATEVER GOD TOLD HIM TO DO, MOSES DID. (IN CHAP. 8:13 & 31 WE READ, 'AND THE LORD DID ACCORDING TO THE WORD OF MOSES.' ANSWERED PRAYER FOLLOWING THE LIFE OF OBEDIENCE). ANYWAY, IT MAGNIFICENTLY ILLUSTRATES THE FACT [THAT] WE ARE TO OBEY (TAKE CARE OF THE POSSIBLE) AND TRUST GOD FOR THE IMPOSSIBLE.

So often Mother admonished us children using those last couple of phrases: *Take care of the possible and trust God for the impossible.* Obey God and then trust him. Do your part, and God will do his part. These were baseline principles by which Mother has tried to live, and for that, her Christian walk has a powerful measure of balance about it. She is practical, *and* she believes God for big things. She can take God very seriously, praying with conviction and stamina, *and* be lighthearted, fun, and humorous, seeing God's hand in the most amusing turns of event. In her balance, I see great freedom—

and I pray I can learn the same for myself.

In many ways, Mother has made faith look easy. I recognize the richness of her relationship with Christ has been hard won. It is impossible, for instance, to know the depth of loneliness she must have experienced during my father's long absences. She made the most of her circumstances and built a life, but I imagine she suffered. Perhaps loneliness is part of what her "boot camp" experience at boarding school prepared her to endure.

And yet the example my mother—and my father—set in loving God so completely no matter the circumstances, losses, or trials has been tremendous. I feel utterly inadequate by comparison. I have not lived a life as yielded to God as my mother. I am stubborn, willful, and independent. I disobeyed my parents at times. I wanted to go my own way. I have done the same with God. I realize this urge toward independence is human. As the Bible says, "All we like sheep have gone astray; we have turned every one to his own way" (Isaiah 53:6, KJV). But I long to bend my will to God's will, even as I have seen Mother do; and I have had such a hard time of it.

In my adult life, I have endeavored to maintain many of the outward disciplines I learned from Mother, particularly those of prayer and Bible study. I have also tried to practice Christ's teachings by reaching out to others as my mother taught me from my earliest years. But Mother's actions of Bible study, prayer, and charity are the visible manifestations of a deeper reality: a personal relationship with Christ and an understanding of his love and sovereignty in all situations.

It is this deeper reality that I long to develop and nurture in my own life. While I may have taken on Mother's disciplines—the "vegetables" she enjoyed while hoping we, too, would enjoy them—more so, I desire to assimilate the foundational truths on which Mother has staked her life. And perhaps chief among these is the truth that God is worthy of our deepest love, surrender, and obedience. May I learn to live out that truth to the fullest!

Mother with my
oldest child,
Noelle

Anne, Gigi, Mother, Franklin, and me (center)

CHAPTER 4

HOMEMAKING

All service ranks the same with God.
ROBERT BROWNING

THE SUMMER SUN was at its zenith as my siblings and I, towels tucked under our arms, ran down the mountain from the house to our swimming hole. Mother was not far behind in the Jeep, bringing a cooler of drinks and a watermelon. Perched on the little grassy knoll beside the swimming hole was one of Mother's "junking" finds, a dilapidated piece of furniture purchased on a recent morning excursion to Asheville.

Junking on summer mornings was Mother's ritual—and, as we were her children, it was ours, too. Mother would load us into the Jeep, or, her good friend, whom we called Aunt

Betty, would take all of us in her station wagon; and we would travel from Montreat into Asheville and neighboring towns, where we haunted junk shops, keeping an eye out for any pieces Mother might want.

Primitive antiques, which Mother preferred, were not in vogue at the time, and most people would have agreed that what Mother purchased was junk. But once Mother got her hands on a broken-down piece of furniture, it was destined to become beautiful and desirable. She saw potential in what others threw away.

As soon as we got to the swimming hole, only a few minutes' run from the house, we jumped in—and the water was about as cold as we could stand it! A very frigid, dammed stream fed our swimming hole, and with the cold water came snakes, frogs, and tadpoles, among other creatures. Whenever it rained—which was many a summer afternoon—someone had to run down to the swimming hole to divert the stream so it wouldn't overflow the pool's banks and deposit an unwelcome layer of leaves and mud on the bottom.

On this day, the sky was clear, and Mother soon appeared at the swimming hole in her bathing suit, carrying a pair of rubber gloves and the tools of one of her favorite trades: furniture refinishing. She eyed her latest project, this one a table, awaiting her on the knoll.

We stayed at the swimming hole all afternoon, rubbing our toes raw on the cement bottom, while Mother worked on the table. She spent hours scraping, taking finish off, sanding, and putting finish back on. The sun beat down on her tanned skin, and every once in a while she would take a quick dip in the pool to cool off. Then she would go right back to her project.

We didn't mind Mother being absorbed in her work—although she wasn't so distracted she couldn't keep her eye on us. We were too busy splashing, howling, and pestering each other. Wisely, Mother had chosen to do her refinishing in an environment where we could have fun, too. Her hobby took nothing away from us. It only added pleasure.

The Highest Calling

Mother taught my sisters and me that a woman's highest calling was to be a wife and mother and to make a home for her family. I never got the sense that Mother felt locked away as a homemaker, or left at home with the baggage while my father traveled. Quite the opposite, I believe she felt fortunate that she could stay at home. Making a home was what Mother enjoyed doing, and she often said as much: "Liberated to stay at home," she would say.

In the case of my mother, she literally made our home. Much has been written—in fact, pieces of the story now take on an almost mythic quality—about Mother's homesteading adventures: How she bought our 150 acres on the mountain while my father was out of town and was met with his now-famous (at least in our family) words upon his return: "You *what?*"

How she worked, assisted by an architect, to design a log cabin-style home and then traversed the region looking for actual log cabins she could purchase so the builders would have ancient lumber to use on the house's interior and exterior.

How rock masons quit on the spot after she told them she wanted walls made of stone without any mortar showing—Mother's idea seemed to compromise the acceptable style of the day.

How carpenters and plasterers balked when she instructed them in the art of making the house look old. One carpenter, on his way out after quitting, is quoted in Mother's biography as having said, "A man can't take no pride in this kind of work." [1] And the stories go on.

For Mother, homemaking was an artistic endeavor. Our home, in many ways, was her canvas. She had a vision for our home, and she was always adding to or embellishing that vision—whether she was buying and refinishing "junk," remodeling an area of the house, or rearranging the furniture in a particular room.

Mother had an eye for beauty. She studied interior design books. She studied furniture. She owned volume after volume on New England homes, early American furniture, and a host of other decorating-related subjects. She knew lines. She knew quality. She understood balance and proportion. When she went on her junking runs, she knew what she was looking for.

As she created our environment, Mother particularly emphasized the importance of making a home comfortable. She wanted feather pillows and warm blankets on all the beds, comfortable mattresses, comfortable chairs, and plenty of good reading light. She made sure little bouquets of fresh flowers were set out in the rooms. And our stereo system piped music—hymns or, during the holidays, Christmas carols—throughout the house. Mother put a high premium on atmosphere.

In many ways, Mother recreated on our mountain the safe, happy compound she knew as home in China. She borrowed some specific features from her childhood home—like the swimming hole, for instance—but our home seemed akin to Mother's compound in Tsingkiangpu more in the sense, again, of atmosphere. Safety, happiness—these were the dominant aspects of life at Little Piney Cove. We played games; we held family devotions; we read books; we laughed; we romped in our woods; we were encouraged to use our imaginations. Mother likewise grew up with a sense of security and freedom. She loved her childhood, and I believe she wanted to transfer the gifts of her early experience to us.

I am a primitive.
I love
primordial silences
that reign
unbroken over ridge
and plain,
unspoiled by
civilization's roar.
I love the lonesome sound
of wind,
the final crashing
of a tree,
the wash of waves
upon the shore,
wind, thunder, and
the pouring rain
are symphonies to me.

—Ruth Bell Graham / *Collected Poems,* 213

Parenting

Mother, of course, had wonderful models of godly parents in *Lao E* and *Lao Niang*. Her father was fairly strict but fun, jovial, and energetic—thoroughly engaged with his four children. Her mother kept the home orderly and cheerful, nurturing her children's creativity; establishing traditions; and maintaining a stable, pleasant environment during a time of turmoil and insecurity. As I have written, Mother frequently tells of her parents never showing fear around their children, even while seeing bomb-laden Japanese planes fly overhead.

MOTHER REALLY HAD FEW PARENTING RESOURCES ON WHICH TO DRAW. SHE HAD TO GET HER DIRECTION FROM THE LORD. HER WELFARE—AND OURS—DEPENDED ON HIM, AND SHE UNDERSTOOD THAT.

Mother drew heavily on her parents' example. In my memory, Mother never exhibited fear or anxiety in front of us. She wasn't afraid of snakes or spiders. She wasn't afraid of driving the Jeep up and down our steep mountain drive or plowing snow off the same precarious ascent. She would even plow the steep driveways of neighbors if they needed help. Mother was adventuresome and did not allow unnecessary obstacles to get in her way. She wasn't foolish, but neither was she easily daunted. After all, she built an unorthodox house for her several children on an isolated piece of property atop a difficult-to-access mountain. As a young girl, Mother's dream was to go to Tibet to be a pioneer missionary; as an adult, she managed to do a fair amount of pioneering while rearing us!

Even though Mother could look to her parents while she

was mothering—and she could look to them daily because they lived in Montreat, at the bottom of the mountain—at the same time, given her unique position as the wife of an evangelist of unprecedented renown, Mother really had few parenting resources on which to draw. She had to get her direction from the Lord. Her welfare—and ours—depended on him, and she understood that.

When I started having children, Mother did share with me a book she had referenced when we were growing up called *A Parents' Guide to the Emotional Needs of Children*, by David Goodman. And she told me that she had employed a very simple philosophy in rearing us. In typical "adage" fashion, Mother explained that training children was much like training dogs—reward and praise for obedience, swift and firm punishment for disobedience!

One thing Mother honed to a fine art was her ability to determine what in life was serious or of real concern, thus meriting her energy and attention, and what was not. When it was our turn to rear children, Mother's advice reflected her own practice: "If it's not a moral issue, then let it go." In our growing-up years, long hair and loud music were a couple of the adolescent excesses parents were facing. About such things, Mother might have said, depending on the scenario, "These aren't moral issues—they're not a big deal." However,

Mother did not tolerate disobedience or sassing of any kind; we were to respect our elders and tell the truth. She seemed to know instinctively which battles to fight.

Mother did not need us to make her look good as a parent, and having reared children of my own, I appreciate her sense of security. Some adults need their children to validate them, to perform and achieve in order to reflect well on their parenting efforts. Not so with Mother. She did not make us feel that her reputation was riding on our achievement or lack thereof. She wanted us to succeed in God's purpose for our lives, but we were allowed to be ourselves—or, at least, we were made to believe we could be ourselves! So many other people had expectations of us that Mother did not create added pressure.

Franklin and me

Overall, I might describe Mother as a kind of "laissez-faire" parent. Not that she ignored naughtiness on our part. I can remember one time when maybe three or four of us had misbehaved, and Mother lined us all up against her bed and played us like a xylophone with her flexible shoehorn! Still, while we knew we were being punished, we recognized that Mother was not administering *capital* punishment.

Maybe growing up in a China overrun with bandits caused Mother to conclude that there were some very serious issues against which others paled. Life and death—whether physical or spiritual—were serious. If we were in danger of physical or moral harm, then Mother drew the line. Otherwise, she was pretty relaxed—and in some cases, *very* relaxed. After all, she did let us swim with snakes, albeit non-poisonous ones, and chase each other around like wild people. (Once when chasing Franklin I slipped and sliced my scalp open on the sharp corner of a plaster wall!) Mother rolled with the punches, taking our shenanigans in stride. She took her cues from the Lord and did what she believed best.

"My Job Is to Make You Good"

Mother had great fun with us. Our summer afternoons by the swimming hole were idyllic. I can still see Mother sitting in the yard laboring over a rickety piece of furniture, her skin glistening with perspiration, her brow furrowed as she focused on her task, though not so intently she couldn't abandon it every now and then for her children, the snakes, and the tadpoles.

Even when Mother played with us, though, she maintained her position as our mother. She kept a healthy parental distance. For instance, she taught us to swim, but she did not spend hours swimming with us, as if she were one of us. She was our mother first, and then our friend. She used to quote *Lao Niang* and say, "My job is not to make you happy, but to make you good."

Yet Mother made us happy, too. Every Sunday morning she got up and cooked pancakes and usually a roast for Sunday afternoon dinner. From time to time, Mother would cook Chinese food. She did not often cook during the week; our beloved housekeeper Bea did most of the cooking. Mother had several wonderful people who helped her around the house and property, and these loyal employees freed her up to tend to her many other responsibilities and to have more fun with us.

Not having to do all of the ironing, washing, and grocery shopping, Mother was afforded opportunities to enjoy the less stressful sides of motherhood. She could come downstairs in the morning, have devotions with us, and kiss us as we walked out the door for school. When we got home in the afternoons, she would be standing at the door to greet us, ready to take us on a hike. Mother was very much engaged with the business of our household, but she was fortunate to have secured the invaluable assistance of others; and with my father gone so much, I know she appreciated that help, perhaps more than we will ever know.

Balance

As I look back and consider the way Mother parented us, what strikes me—in this just as in other areas of Mother's life—is her profound sense of balance. She just seemed to know when to do her part and when to look to God to do his; when to take a matter seriously and when to move on. She was introspective and thoughtful, and she was winsome, light-hearted, and fun. She could be strong and determined, and she could be laid-back and easy-going.

When I consider Mother's steadiness—her grounded, levelheaded, if at times whimsical and unpredictable, approach to rearing us—I marvel. Of course, I have the benefit of hindsight. I imagine that while embroiled in the task of rearing us, Mother felt woefully inadequate. In fact, I believe Mother often felt that as a parent she was flying by the seat of her pants. She has written so.

In her book, *It's My Turn*, Mother quotes a journal entry detailing her doubts and feelings:

> I LIE AWAKE NIGHTS LOATHING MYSELF FOR THE PERSON I AM, FEARFUL AND WORRIED THAT I CANNOT BRING UP THIS FAMILY AS I SHOULD. AND I CAN'T.
>
> I AM A WEAK, LAZY, INDIFFERENT CHARACTER; CASUAL WHERE I SHOULD BE CONCERNED, CONCERNED WHERE I SHOULD BE CAREFREE; SELF-INDULGENT, HYPOCRITICAL, BEGGING GOD TO HELP ME WHEN I AM HARDLY WILLING TO LIFT A FINGER FOR MYSELF; QUARRELSOME WHERE I SHOULD BE SILENT, SILENT WHERE I SHOULD BE OUTSPOKEN; VACILLATING, EASILY DISTRACTED AND SIDETRACKED. [2]

How did Mother cope with the overwhelming sense that the task in front of her was too much to handle? She did as the psalmist did—she acknowledged her helplessness and fear, and then she turned to the Lord. "All that I am not, He is; all that I am and should not be, He forgives and covers," she wrote in the same journal entry.

Mother might not have felt any differently, any less overwhelmed, for making a declaration of God's sovereignty in her situation, but, nonetheless, she kept looking to him. She has said that while rearing us, she asked God to overrule her mistakes. Mother knew where her help came from; she knew she had nothing in herself to satisfy the many demands placed on her. And she knew that God's help would come when it was needed. Mother depended on God to be, in the psalmist's words, the strength of her life (Psalm 27:1, KJV). And he was just that—for from the outside, she seemed to carry everything off beautifully.

God,
bless all young mothers
at end of day,
kneeling wearily with each
small one
to hear them pray.
Too tired to rise when done …
and yet, they do,
longing just to sleep
one whole night through.

Too tired to sleep …
too tired to pray …
God,
bless all young mothers
at close of day.

—Ruth Bell Graham / *Collected Poems*, 234

What I Took Away

I borrowed much from mother as I parented my own three children—Noelle, Graham, and Windsor. I took away specific traditions and practices, like family devotions, praying on our knees, and Bible memorization exercises. I tried to pass on to my children a love of God and of the Scriptures. Like Mother, I allowed candy and a soft drink only on Sunday afternoons. We did Christmas much like Mother had done Christmas when I was a child. And, of course, Sunday school and church were non-negotiables.

More generally, I tried to emulate Mother, and, thus, my grandparents, by creating a safe, happy environment for my children. I built my own version of a compound—a ranch in Texas, and later a horse farm in Virginia's Shenandoah Valley— where my children could play to their hearts' content and feel secure. We kept a mini-menagerie that included horses, dogs, cats, fish, a bird, a guinea pig, and any number of reptiles my son, Graham, might hunt down. In Texas, I would take the kids on picnics in the pastures only to startle as snakes slithered by or scorpions scurried under nearby rocks!

Whatever we did, I wanted the kids to have fun and experience adventure. Once I drove for hours taking them to see dinosaur footprints in a Texas streambed. Every summer I loaded up the kids in the station wagon and drove them from Texas to Montreat—a couple of days' drive. I broke up the time by giving the children a little treat each hour, like a box of raisins, some new crayons, or a special cassette tape. I stopped in the evening at a hotel with a pool so we could swim. Afterward, we would have supper and go to bed, and then get back in the car the next morning. This was before cars had seatbelts, so my kids floated around in the backseat, at times wreaking havoc. I kept a wooden spoon in the front seat lest I need to turn around and whack someone who might be transgressing the rules!

I TRIED TO EMULATE MOTHER, AND, THUS, MY GRANDPARENTS, BY CREATING A SAFE, HAPPY ENVIRONMENT FOR MY CHILDREN.

My children have told me they enjoyed the little things I did to generate an atmosphere that promoted both discipline and joy. I know I was pretty relaxed as a parent. Often my philosophy was: "If Mother did it that way, then it must be okay." In some instances, I followed her example quite literally, though perhaps unconsciously.

One scene from our Texas days comes to mind. The kids were playing in the swimming pool, and I asked my husband to move a big, oak, claw-foot table onto the wrap-around porch. I wanted to keep my eye on the kids while I worked on my latest household project: refinishing the table, which I originally had purchased and refinished some years earlier, but which now was scarred and in need of a re-do.

I labored in the shade, working the new finish into the crevices of the claw-feet, while out in the sun the children splashed and squealed, playing their water games. Every now and again, one would shout, "Look, Mom!" And I would glance up from my tedious undertaking, watch a water trick, and compliment the performer. Then I would turn back to my project.

Like Mother on those summer afternoons by the swimming hole, I was spending time with the children, cheering them on and watching out for them, but I was also doing something I needed and wanted to do. I guess this is one of the secrets of homemaking, one Mother perfected: Involving your children in your hobbies or the ongoing habits of the home not just so that life can run smoothly, but also because relationships and memories get built that way, day by day.

I DID WANT MY CHILDREN TO GROW UP LOVING GOD, LOVING PEOPLE, AND KNOWING HOW TO ENJOY LIFE.

Did I do everything right? Absolutely not. Like Mother, I felt terribly inadequate when it came to parenting, homemaking, and the like, and I often believed I was groping in the dark. But I did want my children to grow up loving God, loving people, and knowing how to enjoy life. I suppose only the kids—who are now grown and, in the case of my daughters, rearing children of their own—can say whether I succeeded. I know I sure had fun along the way!

Four generations—
Mother; my
younger daughter,
Windsor; her son;
and me

Mother, 1989

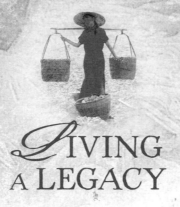

CHAPTER 5

*L*IVING A LEGACY

The lines have fallen to me in pleasant places;
Indeed, my heritage is beautiful to me.

PSALM 16:6

WENDING HIS WAY through the crowded streets of Shanghai, the driver of our private bus followed Mother's directions—given through our translator—turning here and then there, dodging the hordes of bicyclists, and carefully listening to the descriptions Mother pulled out of her memory regarding the location of a Number 4 Quinsan Road.

It was May 1989—just weeks before Chinese government forces massacred pro-democracy demonstrators in Beijing's

Tiananmen Square—and Mother, my two sisters, and I were touring the country. Mother had waited a long time to bring her three daughters to China. Her family left the country during World War II, hoping at some point to return; but they were not able to go back until 1980, when Mother, her brother, and her two sisters were invited by the Chinese government to visit their hometown. By then, Mother was almost sixty years old, and *Lao E* and *Lao Niang* were already gone.

MOTHER... [HAD] BROUGHT US TO SEE THE LAND WHERE *LAO E* AND *LAO NIANG* HAD WORKED FAITHFULLY AS CHRISTIAN MEDICAL MISSIONARIES FOR NEARLY A QUARTER OF A CENTURY.

Mother returned to China again in 1988, the year my father held a series of meetings there. And now, a year later, Mother was back, having brought us to see the land where *Lao E* and *Lao Niang* had worked faithfully as Christian medical missionaries for nearly a quarter of a century.

Ours was a semi-official trip, complete with government-sponsored tours of ancient gardens, historical sites, and even the homes of loyal citizens. The Chinese government also gave Mother leeway to request visits to certain locations, and Number 4 Quinsan Road, formerly the location of a missionary boarding house oft-frequented by Mother's family, was—at least to me—one of the most important of these locations.

The missionary boarding house on Quinsan Road—or, as we soon discovered, Quinsan Gardens—was the site of two of Mother's poignant life memories. It was also the place where

Mother and her family stayed when they traveled in and out of China, and the rooms and halls seemed as familiar to Mother as old friends. Here in this boarding house, lying in bed, Mother, on her way to school in what is now North Korea, had asked God to let her die rather than face separation from her home and parents. Here, too, Mother had once become so sick with a fever that adults had been forced to put her in a tub of ice!

When I was growing up, these powerful moments in Mother's life were some of my bedtime stories, and so, the Shanghai missionary boarding house, where Mother had stayed so many times, became a place where I felt I, too, had stayed. In some way, the boarding house seemed to belong to me, for in my imagination I saw vividly the rooms, my grandparents, the tub of ice, and the young girl praying in her bed.

With these images in my mind now, searching Shanghai for the boarding house became a time of real suspense and anticipation. We had just come from Hong Kong—Shanghai was our first stop on China's mainland— and the boarding house

would be our first significant, personal encounter with the scenes and tales of Mother's childhood in this country.

We waited excitedly as Mother pointed out various turns, speaking to our translator, who then directed the bus driver through the Shanghai neighborhood's crowded streets. Determined to find the house, Mother seemed to remember familiar signposts along the way; and at a certain point, knowing we were close, she signaled to the driver. Making one last turn, we finally saw it: Quinsan Gardens.

Mother's Memories

"There it is! There it is!" we shouted joyfully, collecting our cameras and purses so we could disembark.

On the street, a group of Chinese promptly gathered to see what all of the commotion was about. We stood looking at a four-story, Victorian brick building with large, arched windows. In front of the building, which spanned about the length of a city block, stood a row of stalls housing the wares of local merchants. Bicyclists and pedestrians came and went, while the little knot of onlookers surrounded Mother, eyeing her with curiosity.

Standing on the sidewalk in front of Number 4, Mother began to tell her stories, pointing to the window of the room where she spent the night on her way to boarding school, or

Mother in front of the former
missionary boarding house,
Shanghai

on her way to America with her family. My sisters and I took photographs and listened as our mother talked again of the tub of ice, the prayer to die, the memories of my grandparents.

Watching Mother gesturing toward the building, her face radiant, I felt my eyes brim with tears. I could almost see my grandparents. And hear their voices. My heart was full of longing for them and nostalgia for a time I had never known. This was what I hoped the whole trip would be like: Mother taking us back to the important places in her life and reminiscing with us, walking us through the hallways of her memories, showing us more of herself—and, thus, more of ourselves.

In fact, to me, this experience with Mother in front of the Shanghai boarding house was perhaps the most satisfying of any that followed on our month-long excursion. Later we visited Mother's hometown—on Mother's Day—but we were not able to make the same kind of connection to Mother's childhood. Not only had her childhood home been torn down; but also, walking through the streets, we found ourselves crowded by officials who wanted to steer us in directions other than what Mother had in mind.

Our gathering in front of the Shanghai missionary boarding house, though, was like a wonderful moment outside of time. No officials were leading us. This was our own journey, our own special experience. There had been all of the excitement surrounding Mother's hunt for the boarding house, and then the jubilation when she found it. Standing near Mother as she told her stories, I thought: *Here my loved ones walked and talked and experienced things in an age before I was born. Here memories were made.* I felt as if I was almost re-living the scenes with Mother, and I realized I was beginning to have a sense—a tangible, lived sense—of the power of legacy.

Legacy of Love

One of Mother's purposes in taking us to China was to provide us with a detailed, on-the-ground encounter with the legacy left us by my grandparents and by all who had shared the gospel message in that country. Mother had given us an excellent reading list to prepare us for the trip; and now she was anxious for us to see for ourselves how the seeds my grandparents planted—by taking the gospel to China and serving in the medical field in Christ's name—were bearing fruit even now, even after Mao Zedong's Cultural Revolution, during which Christians were brutally persecuted. Through waves of repression by government forces, the Christian church had survived and thrived. This was one of China's great stories, and we somehow shared a part in it through the legacy of my grandparents and their Christian co-laborers.

In fact, we saw the "fruit" of the Christians' labor in China when we attended church gatherings and could look into the faces of Christian believers, who came out in droves to worship. We also met people whose lives had been touched directly by my grandparents' service in medicine: one whom *Lao E* treated for tonsillitis; a man on whom my grandfather operated when, as a boy, the man was wounded by Japanese shrapnel; a nurse in the hospital where *Lao E* worked; the daughter of my grandparents' cook; one former patient to whom *Lao E* said, "I can heal your leg, but I want you to know the One who can heal your soul."

These people had heard in advance about Mother's visit—the news seemed to have gone out like a drumbeat—and they traveled from out of town, gathering in a conference room at our Shanghai

Lao E, Aunt Virginia, a friend, Lao Niang, Uncle Clayton, and Mother in front of their China home hotel, to greet Dr. Nelson Bell's daughter. Due to his many medical contributions and faithful service, my grandfather was a man of some renown in China. One of the Chinese who came to meet us in Shanghai wanted to travel to America to visit *Lao E*'s grave and even had his passport ready!

Meeting these Chinese who knew *Lao E* and *Lao Niang* brought the reality of my grandparents' legacy home to me in a very specific way. Now, as we conversed with these friends through translators in the hotel conference room, I was profoundly struck by the fact that I was listening to the very people whose lives had been impacted by my grandparents' service, kindness, and love. As tales and memories were recounted, *I* began to feel impacted by my grandparents' love for these people. Love, after all—love for Christ, the Chinese, and foreign missions—was my grandparents' legacy. Love was what *Lao E* and *Lao Niang* had come to China to demonstrate, and that love was still working in the hearts of those touched by it. These people with whom we met may have been strangers in one sense, but in another sense, they seemed familiar—because of the love, God's love, which my grandparents freely gave.

> I WAS PROFOUNDLY STRUCK BY THE FACT THAT I WAS LISTENING TO THE VERY PEOPLE WHOSE LIVES HAD BEEN IMPACTED BY MY GRANDPARENTS' SERVICE, KINDNESS, AND LOVE.

Participants in the Legacy

My sisters and I, however, had come to China to do more than just experience or glimpse the legacy of my grandparents' efforts; our trip was meant to be more than a look-see. We also had come to speak to church groups and share the truth of Scripture. We were in China to *bring* the message of God's love through Christ—the same message my grandparents brought, the same message my father had brought to China the year before we arrived.

I WAS EVER AWARE THAT I WAS PLAYING A PART IN SOMETHING MUCH BIGGER THAN MYSELF.

Not just observers of the legacy, we had traveled to the land of my mother's birth to be participants in that legacy, and as such, I was ever aware that I was playing a part in something much bigger than myself. In some modest way, I was being granted the privilege of contributing to a beautiful history—the history of God's church in a vast, intriguing, diverse, and ancient culture. And for that, I was humbled, awed, and profoundly grateful.

I wondered what Mother must have thought looking on as her daughters shared from the Scriptures with the Chinese believers. Or, going back a little, how must Mother have felt when Daddy first visited China in 1988, the year before our trip?

The sense of being a part of a multi-generational legacy must have been awe-inspiring to her. Mother's parents had committed themselves to ministry in China. Now her husband was bringing the gospel to China. Eventually, her youngest son—my brother, Ned—would become involved in ministry in China. Her daughters and—though not with us on our trip—her oldest son, Franklin, were participating. God was writing his love on the nation Mother loved using the ink of her own bloodline. What an awesome convergence! To see her heart's desire for China being fulfilled by those whom she loved most dearly must have been amazing for Mother.

For as long as I can remember, Mother has modeled an attitude of humility toward the legacy of which she is a part. She considers her contribution just a small piece of some greater work of God. My father's ministry, of course, is much bigger than both of my parents, and Mother has maintained a godly perspective about her role in it. She doesn't think of herself as special for being a part of what God is doing through the ministry, but as privileged and honored. She understands

Anne, Mother, Gigi, and me (far left) at the Great Wall

that she did not do anything to deserve the role in which God placed her—God in his sovereignty simply chose her. She is no more special than anyone else. She is not entitled. And in this posture of humility, Mother has set such a vital example for us, her children.

Mother's Qualities

Traveling around China with Mother—observing her in the context of the culture that formed her—I came to understand with greater clarity some of Mother's quirks and qualities. Even as the trip to the Shanghai missionary boarding house brought stories from Mother's childhood to life; to an extent, simply being with Mother in China gave me greater insight into aspects of her personality that I had taken for granted. I saw the whole woman—or at least more of what made the woman—as I journeyed with Mother in the land of her formative years.

Her Love for Old Things

The more we saw of China, the more I found myself fascinated with the antiquity of Chinese culture, its architecture, and its artifacts. We visited sites that were centuries old, millennia old. One day we went to see a garden older than America.

I particularly remember the sense of awe I experienced

walking atop China's Great Wall. The sky was clear the day we made our trip, and we ended up with a little section of the vast, historic structure all to ourselves. (Mikhail Gorbachev happened to be visiting the wall that day, and the usual throng of tourists had migrated accordingly.) From where we stood, the view of the wall and the surrounding countryside was breathtaking. The wall's history and sheer physical reach seemed almost too much to take in, and I was deeply moved.

As I let my eyes follow the wall where it stretched over the hills to the horizon, I found myself thinking about Mother's love of history. I thought about her love of tradition, the value she places on connection with the past, and her love of old things. Growing up I had seen this love manifest in many ways. Mother's love for old things came out as she created Little Piney Cove—buying hordes of old logs and beams for construction materials; having the builders stylize our home's interior to look old; purchasing old "junk" with which to furnish the house. Mother saw beauty in the old and discarded. She saw value in what other people had abandoned or forgotten. What was simply "old" to some people seemed to have mystery and meaning in Mother's eyes.

I HAVE WATCHED MOTHER ENCOURAGE HURTING PEOPLE, INSISTING THAT THEIR LIVES WERE FAR FROM OVER AND THEIR CONTRIBUTIONS VALUABLE.

I do not know how much of Mother's fondness for what is old can be attributed to China's influence, but I do see ways that God has worked through this aspect of Mother's personality. For Mother does not only see value in old *things*—like the "junk" furniture she brought home and refinished on the lawn beside the swimming hole. Mother sees beauty, too, in people whom others might ignore or overlook, like the elderly, the poor, and the helpless. All of my life, I have watched Mother treat with dignity and respect those whom others might dismiss as worn-out; and I have watched Mother encourage hurting people, insisting that their lives were far from over and their contributions valuable.

Of course, seeing beauty in wreckage is what Christ does when he looks at us: he sees the beauty that he placed inside of us when we were created. If we will let him, he will clean us up and reveal that beauty—enhance it, draw it out. No matter our age or station in life, it is never too late for Christ to work in us, restore us, and call us to a good purpose.

> This is a gentle part of town
> —run down.
> Papers blow about the street,
> people walk on tired feet,
> discount stores, a place to eat,
> hardware, garden stuff and such:
> shabby. No, there isn't much
> to see. And yet,
> here's a part I can't forget.
> It isn't something
> I just feel:
> but folks are folks here,
> folks are real,
> folks are simple,
> folks are kind,
> if you don't buy much

they don't mind.
It's just a gentle part of town
—run down.

Ruth Bell Graham / *Collected Poems*, 176

Her Attention to Detail

As I noticed the level of detail-work in Chinese architecture, the phenomenon of Little Piney Cove began to make more sense to me. In the walls of Chinese gardens, for instance, I took note of entrances in the shapes of dragons, ginger jars, and moons. While we have no moon gates at home on the mountain, Mother nonetheless has been very specific, and similarly fanciful, about the features of our home. She has always given loving attention to detail, knowing just what she wanted, even on the smallest scale.

For example: just to the right of the front door inside our house is a tiny peep-out window with panes of bubbled glass that Mother discovered in an old cabin; and in front of the window is a little shelf displaying a miniature glass candle-holder. In one of the bedrooms, Mother designed an arched fireplace with a little nook inset to its side, a place to put knick-knacks. On a wall of yellow pine running down the hallway to her bedroom, Mother enhanced the pine knots using indelible marker, giving them legs and antennae so they would look like friendly bugs. These kinds of seemingly frivolous details mean something to Mother—her taste includes, even requires, such touches.

Perhaps these are the touches of a poet, for Mother's poetry reveals someone who notices unlikely meaning in the often-overlooked details of the world. Mother doesn't seem to miss anything. She sees what, and who, is around her. She sees patterns in the haphazard elements of her environment. Throughout China I perceived in our surroundings the same sort of teeny, gratuitous details that Mother so appreciates, and I could not help but consider that she must have been somehow influenced in her perceptive nature by Chinese culture.

Her Pack Rat Tendencies

Mother is a notorious pack rat and even wrote a book about it called *Legacy of a Pack Rat* (Oliver Nelson, 1989). She saves everything, and it's a good thing. Daddy never would have been able to assemble his memoirs without the fifty-some-odd boxes of paperwork and memorabilia—representing fifty years of his ministry—that Mother dragged out of the attic.

Traveling with Mother in China, I came to see perhaps why she developed the tendency to save just about anything and everything. For in China in 1989—not to mention the

1920s and '30s when Mother lived there—one did not necessarily have ready access to drug stores and hardware stores. People lived with very little and had to make do with what they had. In an atmosphere of scarcity, suddenly Mother's pack-rat tendencies made sense—and proved necessary for our convenience as we traveled.

For instance, if a hotel supplied us with box lunches, Mother might save the plastic wrapping, a rubber band, or a little piece of string. At first my sisters and I poked fun at Mother, finding her usual habit of saving odds and ends a source of amusement. Until we got to more rural areas of China. Then we found ourselves

asking, "Mother, do you have a piece of string?" I thought Mother had been saving unnecessary trash, but she knew we would be gone for a long time and were a long way from Kmart. She was resourceful, like the Chinese, and she reserved what we needed along the way.

I suppose Mother's tendency to save what others might deem trash is connected to her ability to see value where others see none. In Mother's eyes, most anything can have a use. On a humorous note, she used to say, "No one is useless. They can always serve as a bad example!" As I have written, the old, the discarded, the things and people that seem beyond hope of restoration—these Mother views from a perspective altogether different from most. She sees loveliness in the unlovely, usefulness in the seemingly worthless and insignificant. Hers is a redemptive eye, right down to the minutiae of daily life.

I realize this redemptive way of seeing is part of the legacy my mother leaves to me. And it is part of the same legacy of love passed down by *Lao E* and *Lao Niang*. For God's greatest demonstration of love was Christ's redemptive act of dying on a cross for the sins of the world. Because of what Christ did in love, the unlovely *can* be lovely, the worthless valuable, the broken whole. God is a Restorer. And in Mother's ability to see the kernel of value in the wreckage of life, she has followed God. He fashioned and enabled her to see as he sees, and he used China in the process.

Living the Legacy

Coming away from the China trip, I understood Mother in a more dimensional way than ever before, and I suppose I understood myself better, too. I am my mother's child. Some of her traits I have inherited or adopted. Knowing first-hand some of the sources of Mother's tastes and instincts gives me a deeper appreciation of my own tendencies. I see that China touched me, too, even as I grew up on a remote mountain halfway around the world.

In particular, a love of history that I inherited from Mother—a desire to connect with the past—has a great deal to do with why I settled in Virginia's Shenandoah Valley. *Lao E* and *Lao Niang* were from this area, and when I moved here in 1985, Mother still had extended family in the Valley. When my grandparents went on furlough from their post in Tsingkiangpu, they often returned to the Valley. I have run into people who played with my mother here when she was a little girl, and I can drive past the home where Mother first introduced my grandparents to Daddy. These kinds of intersections with the past bring me great satisfaction and remind me daily that I am part of something bigger than myself: A network of generations. A legacy.

But can I live that legacy? Can I take hold of it and practice it in my daily life, making it my own? Can I love with Christ's love and see with Christ's eyes the people God places in my midst? Can I serve people the way Christ served—selflessly? Can I share Christ with those who do not know him? I fall short so often. I become irritable when I should be patient. I move quickly on from strangers when I should stay and encourage them. I look at others and judge. And yet, even as God used China to develop Mother's personality and mold it into something he could infuse with his own likeness, so I must believe God has used my surroundings, relationships, and life circumstances to do the same thing in me. With God's help I *can* live out the legacy. My part is to look to him and ask for his help.

Wherever we come from, whoever our parents and grandparents, we can all be partakers of the legacy God has prepared for us in Christ. For in Christ, we are all one family with one heavenly Father and one inheritance. We may be unique with unique histories and pedigrees, but God's will for each of us is the same: that we be "conformed to the image of His Son" (Romans 8:29).

I am not my mother. I am not my father. I am not my grandmother or my grandfather. I am who God made *me* to be. Yet God has given me the same legacy of love to carry, albeit in a fashion uniquely suited to me, that he has given other members of my family—and Christians everywhere. In my own way, I, too, can bear Christ's image and share his love with the world. And so can you. You can live God's legacy of love. If you will let God shape you. If you will give your life to him and let him do his work in you.

Mother and me

CHAPTER 6

*A*PPROACHING EVENTIDE

Abide with me, 'tis eventide.

M. LOWRIE HOFFORD

I WAS FEELING OVERWHELMED by my life circumstances this particular, recent winter afternoon. The sky was overcast, the mountain air frigid. By contrast, the cozy atmosphere of my Valley home afforded me many comforts, but I was not comforted. I had received several pieces of difficult news in quick succession, and I felt shaky, unsteady. Anxiety. Fear. Exhaustion. These took hold of me. I knew I needed support of some kind—and from someone who loved me. Otherwise, I felt like I might come apart.

Picking up the phone, I decided to call Mother. Normally, I would not have called her at a time like this. It was not my habit to go to Mother with my problems. I did not want to burden her. She was living with physical limitations and discomforts; she and my father, now in their latter years, still carried ministry responsibilities. I did not want to add to Mother's load or cause her to worry.

Furthermore, as the middle of five children, I was used to playing the peacemaker in the family. I tried to keep from rocking the boat. I did not want to add confusion or stir the waters and risk becoming a source of distress for my parents. I sought to please. The result was that from the time I was very young, I kept my loved ones largely at a distance when I was struggling.

IMMEDIATELY, MOTHER WAS PRESENT TO MY NEED. SHE HEARD THE WORRY IN MY VOICE AND LISTENED ATTENTIVELY AS I TOLD HER WHAT I WAS GOING THROUGH …

And yet, while working on a book project in the months preceding this winter afternoon, I had begun to realize that in my habit of holding back from Mother, I had almost prevented her from *being* a mother. I had not let her know that I needed her; and, therefore, she could not meet me with a mother's love in those moments.

Disheartened by this revelation, I no longer wanted to shortchange Mother, or myself—I wanted our relationship to be as rich as it possibly could be. In the stress of my present circumstances, I now thought, *I am going to call Mother. I want to share this with her. I need her prayers.*

Mother answered the phone and greeted me warmly. We spent a few moments catching up on the happenings at Little Piney Cove. Mother shared some news about Daddy and my siblings, just as she always did. I tried to pay attention and respond, but I was having trouble concentrating. Finally, I collected myself and said:

"Mother, I need you to pray about something."

Immediately, Mother was present to my need. She heard the worry in my voice and listened attentively as I told her what I was going through, how helpless I felt, and how the stress was affecting me. I explained that I had no control over my circumstances and that I needed her to pray. Again, I urged her, "Mother, please pray for me. I need prayer."

Lovingly, Mother assured me that I could count on her, and then she settled my repeated petitioning with a simple, humorous remark.

"Well," she quipped cheerfully, "while I'm stuck here on my glue board, at least I can pray!"

Modeling Grace

I reflected on Mother's "glue board" comment for days. On the surface, the comment was typical of Mother: it evoked her sense of levity; it was cute, creative, and surprising. By saying she was stuck on her "glue board," she was referring to her very limited mobility. For the most part, due to painful degenerative arthritis, she is confined to a reclining chair or her wheel chair. I wondered who else I knew could have come up with such a zany metaphor in the face of Mother's circumstances.

But lighthearted as her remark might have been, the implications of the "glue board" metaphor were quite serious. I considered all of the losses Mother is suffering as she ages. My mother was always very independent—and now she has lost her independence. She has always been a very private person—and now, surrounded by caregivers, she has lost much of her privacy. Throughout her life she was an avid reader—and now she can only read with great difficulty. Mother has become intimately acquainted with the privations of old age,

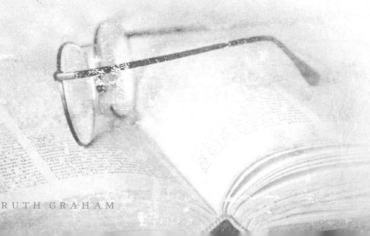

and those privations, which break my heart, seemed to come cascading into my consciousness with Mother's "glue board" comment.

Not that Mother in any way intended her comment to be burdensome to me. On the contrary, Mother was making *light* of her condition. This has been Mother's way of bearing up under suffering. She used to say that she did not want to be a person who gave "organ recitals." And she doesn't give them. I cannot recall ever hearing her complain of physical pain, though were it not for medication, her every move would involve pain. She rarely expresses a need unless prompted by others. Mother is enduring her latter years—she is approaching eventide—with grace, humor, patience, and thoughtfulness. She sits on her "glue board" praying for other people and thinking up ways she can help them. Every time I see or talk to her she wants to know what she can do for me. Considering her condition, I find my mother's selflessness nothing short of amazing.

Another thing I so admire about Mother at this stage is the way she takes care of herself. She has not let herself go. She has not used physical debilitation as an excuse to get sloppy. In the mornings, she puts on her pearl earrings and a pearl necklace. She visits the beautician regularly to have her hair done. She keeps fresh flowers in her room.

Several years ago, my sister Gigi and some others took Mother to the hospital in an ambulance, and, as the story goes, Mother wouldn't get out until she had put on her lipstick! My family members laugh affectionately when this story is told. It is a cute story. But it also reflects the high value Mother places on dignity, and I am so glad she is setting that example. She is modeling grace and elegance, even in one of the most inelegant periods of life.

Mother also takes care to maintain her acumen and mental agility. She keeps her mind sharp and engaged, ever seeking to find ways around her limitations so that she can keep learning. She cannot read very well, but she will sit bent over her Bible with eyeglasses and a magnifying lamp, faithfully studying the Scriptures. Recently, her secretary began typing up, in large font, portions of Scripture that Mother is trying to memorize, in keeping with her lifelong habit of committing chunks of the Bible to memory.

HER CHARACTER HAS ENORMOUS DEPTH AND CONTINUITY. SHE HAS BEEN TESTED AND REFINED BY LIFE, AND SHE HAS PASSED WITH FLYING COLORS.

Mother spends a good bit of time, too, watching video classics and news programs on television, and she pays close attention to current events. When I was lately at home, Mother was absorbed watching the movie *Chariots of Fire*, based in part on the life of Eric Liddell, an Olympic runner from Scotland who, following in his parents' footsteps, became a missionary to China—and later died there in a Japanese internment camp after the bombing of Pearl Harbor.

In between Mother's multiple viewings of the film, she would sit surrounded by scraps of paper that bore her notes in a large, scrawling hand, and she would use her glasses and magnifying light to read from a history of Great Britain. She said she wanted to learn more about the characters in the movie and the narrative's historical backdrop.

Considering Mother's response to suffering and loss—her determination, winsomeness, and fortitude—I think back to the lessons she took care to teach me with such emphasis and passion over the course of my life. She taught me to "count the hours that shine"—to focus on the positives in life and de-emphasize the negatives. In my school days when I was homesick, she urged me not to gripe, but to cultivate cheerfulness. She instructed me that when I felt miserable, I was to find others who were more miserable than I and cheer them up. She showed me how to lean on God and develop a life of personal devotion to him. Now, as I examine Mother's present life, I see she is still practicing all of these principles. Her disciplines are authentic. Her character has enormous depth and continuity. She has been tested and refined by life, and she has passed with flying colors.

When my Fall comes
I wonder
Will I feel
as I feel now?
glutted with happy memories,
content
to let them lie
like nuts
stored up against the coming cold?
Squirrels always gather
so I'm told
more than they will ever need;
and so have I.

Will the dry,
bitter smell of Fall,
the glory of the
dying leaves,
the last brave rose
against the wall,
fill me with quiet ecstasy
as they do now?

Will my thoughts turn
without regret,
to the warm comforts
Winter brings
of hearth fires,
books,
and inner things
and find them nicer yet?

Ruth Bell Graham / *Collected Poems*, 92-93

Nurturing Joy

I don't like to see my mother aging. I don't like to see it because she has always seemed so youthful. Some people say that you fear seeing your parents age because the process speaks of your own mortality, but I can honestly say that my distaste for Mother's condition is, for the most part, not about me. It is about her. I hate to see her limited. The huge scope of her life has narrowed so. Her world seems so small, and I do not like that for Mother.

I remember when Mother drove off the side of the mountain with the friend whom she was trying to cheer up. Mother ordered that stop sign to be put in the ravine as a little joke to make light of the situation, but truly, that accident marked the beginning of the end of her independence. Afterward, we began to question whether she should be driving at all, or staying at the house alone. The whole affair deeply saddened me.

Still, when I remember my mother after she has gone on to be with God, my primary memories are not going to be of her sitting on her "glue board." I will remember her vibrancy, her life, her enthusiasm, and her joy, which she cultivates despite her limitations.

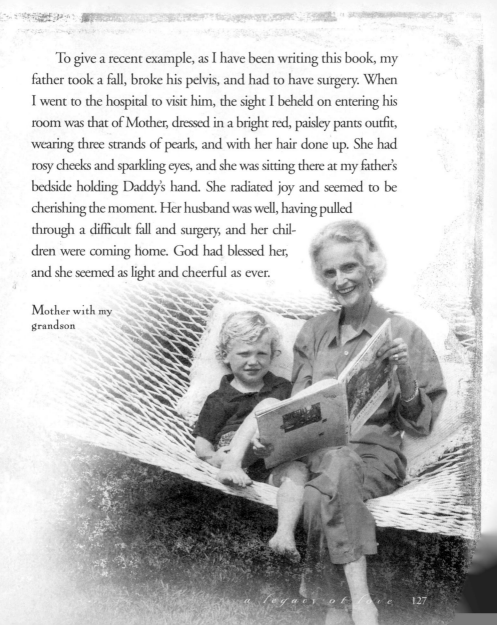

To give a recent example, as I have been writing this book, my father took a fall, broke his pelvis, and had to have surgery. When I went to the hospital to visit him, the sight I beheld on entering his room was that of Mother, dressed in a bright red, paisley pants outfit, wearing three strands of pearls, and with her hair done up. She had rosy cheeks and sparkling eyes, and she was sitting there at my father's bedside holding Daddy's hand. She radiated joy and seemed to be cherishing the moment. Her husband was well, having pulled through a difficult fall and surgery, and her children were coming home. God had blessed her, and she seemed as light and cheerful as ever.

Mother with my
grandson

On another visit home, this one just before Daddy's surgery, I shared a particularly fun moment with Mother—one that revealed her usual whimsy, which had not been dampened even in the face of my father's crisis. The story involves an encounter with critters.

OFTEN WE NEED TO NURTURE THE HABIT OF JOY OVER TIME, AND THROUGHOUT HER LIFE, MY MOTHER WORKED HARD TO DO THAT.

When my siblings and I were growing up, we lived in the midst of a menagerie. Mother loved animals, and we had enough to entertain several families. Some animals, however, were to remain strictly out of doors—and among these, without question, were snakes. They were okay in our swimming hole, but not in the house.

Where poisonous snakes were concerned, Mother, in fact, was a famous snake killer. On our mountain hikes, she always carried her notorious marshmallow fork should the need arise to pin the head of a menacing reptile to the ground in order to clobber it with a rock. Snake killing was a violent activity, but Mother would brook no chances of harm coming to her children.

On my visit home around the time of Daddy's fall, however, I saw another side of Mother regarding her attitude toward snakes. One afternoon I was entering the upstairs hallway from my bedroom and happened upon what looked like a long, black piece of rope on the floor. On first glance, I thought I might be looking at a rubber snake, perhaps left as a practical joke by one of the caregivers. But on closer examination, I discovered this long black "rope" stretched across the wood floor was, indeed, a real snake!

Complicating matters, within the same hour, a housekeeper changing the bed in the room next to mine made a startling discovery: a mother mouse and her five babies were nesting in the sheets! When we came to Mother with the news of a critter invasion, she laughed, eyes shining, and stretched out her hand, gleefully asking to see the baby mice. Of the snake, she said, quite matter-of-factly, "Oh, let him be. We *want* him to be looking for mice!"

I wondered, *Is this my mother?* The snake-and-company's being indoors didn't seem to bother her in the least. On second thought, I realized, the response was actually typical of Mother—her practical jokester side, that is. She got a thrill out of all the commotion.

I can imagine it would be difficult to manufacture the habit of joy overnight in one's latter years. Though God certainly can give us joy whenever we need it, practicing joy can be hard enough when your body is intact, let alone when it begins betraying you. Often we need to nurture the habit of joy over time, and throughout her life, my mother worked hard to do that.

In difficult times, Mother made the decision to count the shining hours. She clung to God when things went wrong, when she was hurting, when her loved ones suffered. She learned to draw on God's peace during times of uncertainty. She learned how to praise him, love him, take comfort in his presence, and apply his Word to her life. She understood what to take seriously and what to let go. She tapped into the mirth of God and appreciated his creation. She learned to see others through God's eyes. She let God teach her how to love selflessly, and in loving so, she learned freedom.

[MOTHER] LEARNED TO DRAW ON GOD'S PEACE DURING TIMES OF UNCERTAINTY . . . SHE LET GOD TEACH HER HOW TO LOVE SELFLESSLY, AND IN LOVING SO, SHE LEARNED FREEDOM.

By doing all of these things, Mother was both nurturing and safeguarding her joy. The Bible says, "the joy of the LORD is your strength" (Nehemiah 8:10). If we can maintain joy in God, then we can maintain strength during our tough times. Perhaps this is another part of the legacy Mother has passed on to me: the ability to choose joy regardless of circumstances, and to hang on to that joy when storms come— even as they came in my own life that recent winter afternoon when I picked up the phone and called my mother for help.

An Image of Legacy

I distinctly remember a particular scene from one of my visits home in recent years. I was not witness to the scene—

one of my parents' caregivers told me the story—but somehow, I felt as if I had experienced it myself. I had seen the same picture so many times before.

I learned of the scene early one morning. I had gone downstairs for a cup of coffee and bumped into the nighttime caregiver in the hallway. She told me of something that had happened the previous night.

As I recall from her story, this caregiver had been up late in the evening checking on my parents. On her way to see about my father, she glanced into Mother's room to make sure all was well. The room was dimly lit by a fire—burnt down to embers at this point—and probably by a soft lamp on Mother's 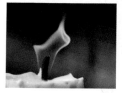 desk. A fragrant candle, too, was burning. The half-canopy bed, dressed in white with touches of blue, was turned back.

Once the caregiver's eyes adjusted to the light, she was startled by what she saw: Bent over on her knees beside the bed—her frail, delicate frame swallowed by a long gown—was my mother. Leaning against the side of the bed, arms folded in front of her, Mother did not move. She was communing with God, worshiping the One she adored, totally unaware of the caregiver's presence in the doorframe.

When the caregiver described this picture of Mother, she looked at me and held my gaze. We both understood the import of the scene. Mother was in poor health, her body as vulnerable and frail as a kitten's. We recognized what kneeling must have required of her. She who had every excuse in the book *not* to get down on her knees, she who knew intense pain as an ever-present reality, had somehow in her frailty mustered the strength to get down from her bed to the floor in order to worship God in the same manner she had done so for most of her life.

I will never forget this image of Mother, seen through the eyes of the caregiver. It is a picture of a woman who, though weak in body, possesses tremendous inner strength and commitment. A woman who loves God more than she loves herself. Who knows and loves him intimately. Whose utmost desire is to be with him. As I think of it now, the image of Mother's tiny frame kneeling there at the side of her bed— where God has spoken to her for the better part of her lifetime and where she has spoken to God—is perhaps the ultimate image of the legacy she leaves to me. For it is an image of love. Her love. And God's love.

No, I will never forget it.

A Legacy of Love

Mother and Daddy with Franklin, Anne, Gigi, and me (on Daddy's lap)

And when I die
I hope my soul ascends
slowly, so that I
may watch the earth receding
out of sight,
its vastness growing smaller
as I rise,
savoring its recession
with delight.
Anticipating joy
is itself a joy.
And joy unspeakable
and full of glory
needs more
than "in the twinkling of an eye,"
more than "in a moment."

Lord, who am I to disagree?
It's only we
have much to leave behind;
so much . . . Before.
These moments
of transition
will, for me, be
time
to adore.

—Ruth Bell Graham / *Collected Poems*, 162

Notes

Chapter 1

1. Annie Fellows Johnston, "The Coming of the Bride," *The Little Colonel Maid of Honor*. http://www.littlecolonel.com/Books/MaidofHonor/Chapter07.htm (October 12, 2004).

2. Ruth Bell Graham, *It's My Turn* (Old Tappan, New Jersey: Fleming H. Revell, 1982), 38.

3. Ruth Bell Graham, *Ruth Bell Graham's Collected Poems*. (Grand Rapids, Mich: Baker Books, a division of Baker Publishing Group, 1977, 1992, 1997, 1998), 7.

Chapter 2

1. Ruth Bell Graham, *It's My Turn* (Old Tappan, New Jersey: Fleming H. Revell, 1982), 18.

2. Patricia Daniels Cornwell, *A Time for Remembering: The Ruth Bell Graham Story* (New York: Harper & Row, 1983), 30.

Chapter 4

1. Patricia Daniels Cornwell, *A Time for Remembering: The Ruth Bell Graham Story* (New York: Harper & Row, 1983), 118.

2. Ruth Bell Graham, *It's My Turn* (Old Tappan, New Jersey: Fleming H. Revell, 1982), 104.

Photo Credits

Cover photograph
>by Russ Busby

Chapter 1
>*Page 6*: Photograph by Bob Cronstedt
>*Page 25*: Photograph by Don Young

Chapter 2
>*Page 30*: Photograph by Russ Busby

Chapter 3
>*Page 54*: Photograph by June Glenn
>*Page 57*: Photograph by Russ Busby
>*Page 71*: Photograph by Russ Busby

Chapter 4
>*Page 72*: Photograph by June Glenn
>*Page 82*: Photograph by Luverne Gustafson
>*Page 91*: Photograph by Tim Barnwell

Chapter 5
>*Page 92*: Photograph by Maury Scobee
>*Page 97*: Photograph by Maury Scobee
>*Page 103*: Photograph by Maury Scobee
>*Page 115*: Photograph courtesy of Missions Children's Hospital, Asheville, NC

Chapter 6
>*Page 116*: Photograph courtesy of Missions Children's Hospital, Asheville, NC
>*Page 127*: Photograph by Tim Barnwell
>*Page 133*: Photograph by June Glenn

Reflections

I WAS TO FILL THE BOOK WITH "CHOICE
TIDBITS" AND "POTENT PHRASES," SHE
EXPLAINED—WHATEVER STUCK IN MY
MIND AND MADE ME THINK.

Reflections

At Inspirio we love to hear from you
—your stories, your feedback,
and your product ideas.
Please send your comments to us
by way of e-mail at
icares@zondervan.com
or to the address below:

inspirio

Attn: Inspirio Cares
5300 Patterson Avenue SE
Grand Rapids, MI 49530

If you would like further information
about Inspirio and the products we
create please visit us at:
www.inspiriogifts.com

Thank you and God bless!